Jay W. Roberts reminds us with teaching: 'no risk, no reward.' An indispensable book and a must read for every educator.
> —**Karlyn Crowley**, Provost, Ohio Wesleyan University

Risky Teaching: Learning to Embrace Uncertainty breaks new ground on a familiar question: is the risk worth it? More than a detached call for educators and institutions to embrace risk, discomfort, and challenge, this book achieves a narrative tone that is both aspirational and practical. Personal reflections give context to the research, and this relatable tone makes it a powerful resource for education leaders at all levels.
> —**Andy Mink**, Vice President for Education, the National Humanities Center

In *Risky Teaching*, Jay W. Roberts acts as a guide to uncertainty as it may surface in teaching, learning, leadership, assessment, and other topics, inside the classroom and in the wider world. Roberts provides the quintessential attitude conferred by a deep immersion in the liberal arts. He is not telling us the one best way to do anything, not out to squash uncertainty or eliminate risk and replace them with recipes that are sure to work. Rather, he reports on many approaches, with their pluses and minuses, and gives us guidance on how they may work for the actual students we work with.
> —**Theo Kalikow**, President Emerita at the University of Maine at Farmington and mentor with the American Council on Education

Risky Teaching

Risky Teaching examines the roles of risk and uncertainty in teaching and learning in higher education. Discussing the current landscape of higher education and the challenges and opportunities we face, this book synthesizes a range of evidence-based and high-impact practices both in and out of the classroom, offering practical strategies and thought-provoking ideas on educational innovation for students and faculty.

Covering topics such as risk-taking inside the classroom, innovative teaching methods outside the classroom, rethinking assessment, and sustaining creativity as we grow in our careers, this practical resource is for faculty and instructors to work within and through uncertainty. The book also explores the inward challenges and opportunities associated with risky teaching and how institutional leaders can encourage productive risk-taking throughout the organization.

This important text is for faculty and instructors in higher education who want to help their students thrive in a complex, unscripted, and disruptive world.

Jay W. Roberts is Provost and Dean of the Faculty at Warren Wilson College, USA

Risky Teaching

Harnessing the Power of Uncertainty in Higher Education

Jay W. Roberts

NEW YORK AND LONDON

First published 2022
by Routledge
605 Third Avenue, New York, NY 10158

and by Routledge
2 Park Square, Milton Park, Abingdon, Oxon, OX14 4RN

Routledge is an imprint of the Taylor & Francis Group, an informa business

© 2022 Taylor & Francis

The right of Jay W. Roberts to be identified as author of this work has been asserted by him in accordance with sections 77 and 78 of the Copyright, Designs and Patents Act 1988.

All rights reserved. No part of this book may be reprinted or reproduced or utilised in any form or by any electronic, mechanical, or other means, now known or hereafter invented, including photocopying and recording, or in any information storage or retrieval system, without permission in writing from the publishers.

Trademark notice: Product or corporate names may be trademarks or registered trademarks, and are used only for identification and explanation without intent to infringe.

Library of Congress Cataloging-in-Publication Data
Names: Roberts, Jay W., author.
Title: Risky teaching : harnessing the power of uncertainty in higher education / Jay W. Roberts.
Description: New York, NY : Routledge, 2022. | Includes bibliographical references and index.
Identifiers: LCCN 2021019968 (print) | LCCN 2021019969 (ebook) | ISBN 9780367461508 (hardback) | ISBN 9780367465957 (paperback) | ISBN 9781003029809 (ebook)
Subjects: LCSH: College teaching. | Education, Higher–Study and teaching. | Risk–Sociological aspects. | Educational innovations.
Classification: LCC LB2331 .R63 2022 (print) | LCC LB2331 (ebook) | DDC 378.1/25–dc23
LC record available at https://lccn.loc.gov/2021019968
LC ebook record available at https://lccn.loc.gov/2021019969

ISBN: 978-0-367-46150-8 (hbk)
ISBN: 978-0-367-46595-7 (pbk)
ISBN: 978-1-003-02980-9 (ebk)

DOI: 10.4324/9781003029809

Typeset in Perpetua
by Apex CoVantage, LLC

To my parents, who taught me to make the risky pass.

Contents

Preface   x
Acknowledgments   xvi

PART ONE
Our Uncertain World   1

1   Introduction   3

2   Uncertainty in Higher Education   16

3   Students and Uncertainty   36

4   Faculty and Uncertainty   57

PART TWO
Teaching Through Uncertainty   75

5   The Uncertain Classroom   77

6   Uncertainty Beyond the Classroom   97

7   Assessing Uncertainty   114

8   Leadership and Uncertainty   133

Index   149

Preface

What to do? I had just finished lunch at a small, rustic cafe in Copenhagen where I had dined on a Danish speciality—Smørrebrød, a type of open-faced sandwich on rye bread, and I had an afternoon to kill. I was in Copenhagen with a colleague of mine in politics leading a May term course titled "Sustainable Cities of Europe." We had left the students to their own devices for the afternoon after a morning tour with the Danish Architecture Center. I had no plans and little idea of what to do or where to go. But I did have a bike, and the weather, while brisk, was inviting enough to consider spending the rest of the day outside. Copenhagen is well-known for its biking culture and infrastructure. Coming from the United States, I was simply astonished to see the sheer number of cyclists and the ease with which they could navigate the city on a bike. My colleague, who had a lot more experience with the city than I did, remarked that the city was "so much smaller" once you had a bike. I was about to discover that for myself.

What is interesting when you are presented with an open-ended task, such as how to spend an afternoon, is what it does to your sense of engagement. I am a fan of tours (as long as they are relatively short). You can gain a lot from listening to a local expert explaining the ins and outs of a particular architectural style or how the city manages its rainwater runoff. Yet, there is also a passive quality to it. There is a lot of information coming at you, and we all have a tendency to tune in and out depending on the situation. In my case, I noticed a pair of sea kayakers making their way down the harbor and disengaged for a time to watch them. "What kind of paddle is that?" I asked myself. "It looks like a traditional wood paddle. Nice." Then I was back to listening to our guide. At another point, an adorable child ambled by, speaking what I assumed was Danish and chasing after a balloon that had blown away in the breeze. "That's so cute," I thought. And then I thought briefly of my wife and kids and how much I missed them. Then, I snapped back into the monologue of the guide as he finished explaining the green roof system on the building in front of us.

PREFACE

The way I was engaging on the tour is fairly typical, I think. When we are in the process of learning something, we move through different modes—passive listening, active listening, active experimentation, and so on. We can in fact learn from simply listening, but it does have its limitations. Anyone who has been on a tour that drags on (and on) with a not-so-engaging guide can attest to the soul-crushing elements of a tour done badly. Luckily, our tour was not that—just 2.5 hours along the harbor front on bikes. I liked it, and so did the students.

But here I was, after lunch, with a bike and an entire city in front of me. What was I to do? I chose to ignore the map on my phone and simply follow my whims. That open exploration of the city is a memory I will cherish for a long time, and as I write this amid the global pandemic, it remains the last time I traveled beyond the borders of the United States. Around every corner was a new discovery—a fountain quietly located in a small park behind a hedgerow. A wonderful promenade along the waterfront with views that stretched for miles. A lovely little bakery with delicious muffins and coffee on the corner of a narrow street. All of this was unplanned and unstructured. There was no guide detailing every last feature or explaining to me what was to come next. Around each corner was an unknown, and my entire being felt engaged, curious, and completely in the moment.

It wasn't all rosy. At one point, I was blissfully biking down a gravel path through a city park when I picked up grumpy stares and shakes of the head from locals as I passed by. I kept biking and soon figured out that bikes were not permitted on the path—whoops! At another point, I followed a narrow street that looked inviting and exited onto a busy street that had me disoriented. Wasn't I just here? How could I have gone in a complete circle? My heart rate went up a notch, and I felt that slight bit of panic at the prospect of being lost (or "temporarily misplaced" as I often say to my wife when she wonders why we just don't stop and ask for directions). I thought about my options and chose to take the busier road for a few blocks to see if things began to look more familiar. It took 10 minutes, but eventually the road brought me back to a landmark I recognized.

The entire afternoon went by in a blur. I was in that sweet spot of open-ended discovery and exploration that we love as human beings, challenging enough to keep me on my toes. Biking in a city like Copenhagen is a joy, but it takes some getting used to. It was novel for me, but not threatening or overwhelming. I was engaged and excited. And I found myself asking lots of questions as I went—what was that guard doing over there—is that an embassy? How come some of the shops are closed today—is it a national holiday? I wonder where that street goes? How far away from my hotel have I biked? Should I try to get home before rush hour? What is rush hour even like on bikes?

This is a book about risk and uncertainty and about the productive roles they play in teaching and learning. In many ways, it is also a memoir of sorts—an attempt to distill 25 years of teaching experience into some kind of a conceptual mold that can hold it all together. As I look back on my career working with

PREFACE

young adults, I return time and time again to this animating vision of what it looks like when the mind, the body, and the spirit are fully engaged in learning. It is a difficult thing to pin down. Teachers often talk about watching "the lightbulb" come on for a student, or they may notice a "sparkle in the eye." We have research that suggests so-called high-impact practices (HIPs) are one category of learning that we might call engaging—things like internships, projects, and small discussion seminars. We also have other literature touting the benefit of certain kinds of methodologies—active learning, game-based learning, and the like. Yet more writing and research argue for the effectiveness of immersive experiences, off-campus study programs, and community-engaged learning. In my 25 years in higher education, I have experimented with many of these approaches and even claimed, in a previous book, that they are all, at the core, various forms of what I would call "experiential education."

Yet, in my visits to a variety of campuses both in the United States and abroad, I have often found faculty and administrators tripping over the terminology. Either they wanted to "get it right" and know for certain whether their teaching adhered to a fill-in-the-blank pedagogical approach, or they would hear a triggering word like "experiential" and sense some amount of judgment about their own teaching style and approach. I found myself spending time trying to delineate artificial boundaries between active learning and project-based learning, for example. Boundaries that, in my mind, were mostly superfluous and irrelevant. I started distrusting the jargon and feeling more than a little empathy with my skeptical audiences as I trotted out yet another term to explain what engaged learning looks like.

On the flight home after one such campus visit and workshop, I let my mind wander as I stared outside the window at 30,000 feet. What was it about that simple turn of a word from "experience" to "experiential" that was so problematic? Was there something deeper, more central to the concept of engaged learning that needed articulation? My background as a student and scholar of John Dewey led my musings back to his notion of the "indeterminate situation." Maybe there is something to this idea of indeterminacy and learning that will help me, I thought. Once back in my office, I went to the bookshelf and pulled out one of the texts that was central to my dissertation, Martin Jay's *Songs of Experience*. And there, on page 292, was what I had been looking for. Jay had been making a claim about Dewey's epistemology on experimentation and certainty and wrote,

> Rather than certainty purged entirely of contingent belief, the goal is increased probability, which involves a perpetual risk of being disproved in the future. Implicitly drawing attention to the "peril" embedded in the etymology of experience, Dewey would argue that "the distinctive characteristic of practical activity, one which is so inherent that it cannot be eliminated, is the

uncertainty that attends it. Of it, we are compelled to say: Act, but act at your peril. Judgment and belief regarding actions to be performed can never attain more than a precarious probability."

(Jay, 2005, p. 292)

In rereading this passage, something clicked for me. Earlier in the book, Jay argues that the etymology of the term "experience" has within it notions of risk and peril. And, he connects that with the way Dewey argues for an epistemology based fundamentally on the concept of uncertainty. Uncertainty *both* in the act of knowledge attainment itself *and* in its aftermath. We are left in the end, according to Dewey, with only "precarious probability."

Experience and its modern manifestation in the discourse of experiential learning are ultimately about these attendant concepts of risk and uncertainty. I thought about many of the most powerful, effective, and transformative teaching and learning environments that I have been a part of. Almost all of them involved risk and uncertainty in various forms. I closed the book and reshelved it, and the idea for this book was born. Three years later, as I write these words looking back on my exploration of risk and uncertainty in teaching and learning, it has been quite a journey. I have read books, articles, and blogs on risk. I have talked to a range of folks—from religious scholars and philosophers to business faculty and psychologists about various notions of uncertainty. I have reflected on my own journey both as a teacher and, now, as an administrative leader in higher education. The result of this work is the book you are reading. My hope is that these ideas and explorations inspire your own thinking on the roles of risk and uncertainty in teaching and learning. In the end, I believe, as with my open-ended bike ride through the streets of Copenhagen, that our experiences with teaching and learning are ours to discover and make. May yours be filled with adventure and just the right amount of risk and uncertainty, and, perhaps, a nice Danish pastry and espresso thrown in along the way.

BOOK ORGANIZATION

The book is organized into two parts. Part One, "Our Uncertain World," sets the context for how risk and uncertainty play out in higher education by exploring these themes through the perspective of both students and faculty and the sector as a whole. The introductory chapter and the one that follows set the stage for the conversation—framing and defining risk and uncertainty and illustrating how, in this particular moment, these concepts are worth considering and practicing. Chapter 2, in particular, discusses these concepts in light of the higher education sector and the unprecedented level of uncertainty and disruption we are experiencing. Technological, demographic, economic, and cultural forces have all contributed to significant disruption and uncertainty for colleges

PREFACE

and universities, and that was all *before* Covid-19. Risk and uncertainty are now the new normal.

Once the broader context of risk has been framed, Chapters 3 and 4 go straight to the heart of the higher education enterprise by focusing on students and faculty. Chapter 3 explores contemporary students and what we are learning about their attitudes, preferences, and ideas, acknowledging that there is no universal single student profile that encapsulates a generation. Nonetheless, it is worth exploring who our students are today and how they perceive risk and learning in their college and classroom experiences. Chapter 4 explores the inward perspectives and dynamics of risk and uncertainty for faculty. Trying new things in (and out) of the classroom takes courage. To be a risky teacher requires a combination of self-awareness, emotional intelligence, confidence, humility, and external support. What can help us, as teachers, take more risks alongside our students? How can we stay creatively restless as we grow into our careers? I will use examples from my own journey through teaching, as well as elements from across the spectrum of thinking on professional development and lifelong learning to discuss best practices for risky teachers.

Part Two, "Teaching Through Uncertainty," focuses more directly on how we might incorporate risky teaching and learning through a variety of methods and approaches. Chapter 5 examines how teachers can intentionally incorporate risk and uncertainty in the classroom. Using principles from a range of authors and my own experiences in teaching, we will explore how we can design for risk and productive uncertainty on the scale of a course, the unit, and the lesson plan. A significant obstacle to this work, in my experience, has been a reluctance for those of us who teach undergraduates to let go of a rather slavish devotion to content. I will discuss the need to take a risk and move away from "content coverage" and describe several examples of what this looks like in different disciplinary approaches. Team-based learning, project- and problem-based learning, and active learning in general all require a certain amount of risk-taking by both instructors and students. We will also explore strategies for setting up an effective classroom culture for risk-taking, as well as the facilitation skills necessary to support learning.

Chapter 6 posits that one of the riskiest things we can do as teachers is leave the lectern, desk, and classroom behind and take students out into the community. Community-engaged learning, place-based learning, service learning, and off-campus study are all recognized methodologies that take students out of the classroom and into the world at large. In addition, the rising influence of the co-curriculum in student learning outcomes requires a deeper integration beyond the classroom walls. Taking these risks with students requires a set of skills, methods, and perspectives beyond those used in the traditional classroom. But, the potential for transformative and powerful learning can make the risk worth the reward.

Chapter 7 explores every teacher's favorite topic—assessment. As we explore risky forms of teaching and learning, how do we adjust our understanding and expectation of assessment? Often, grading and grades can represent a significant obstacle to faculty as they work with productive uncertainty in teaching and to students as they are learning. There are strategies and methods to help address this, and we will explore ways to move beyond the culture of one right answer and learn to embrace failure as part of the teaching and learning process.

In the final, concluding chapter, I discuss risk on the scale of the institution and institutional leadership. As we live through this uncertain time in higher education, what does it mean for the institution and the institutional leader to embrace risk and uncertainty? What examples, case studies, and lessons learned exist to help us navigate a sector and a world filled with uncertainty and its attendant risks? How can institutional leaders and administrators support faculty and students in the classroom and in the community and help them to embrace uncertainty and take action in ways that improve learning, enhance outcomes, and serve broader educational and societal aims?

Acknowledgments

There are many people to acknowledge for their support of this project. I would like to especially thank my colleagues at Earlham College and at Warren Wilson College for their support, encouragement, and hard work, which allowed me the space I needed to get this project done. In particular, Hillie, Carol, and Gary—I could not have done this without you. You helped onboard me to a new campus and community and offered the kind of support and leadership that enabled me to spend the time necessary to finish this project. To my wife and daughters: You have heard me talk about this book over many meals, trips, and weekends, and you admirably tolerated my mild obsessions with these topics over the last three years. You also saw a little less of me from time to time than I would have liked as a result, and I hope you know that this book is as much your accomplishment as mine in the many ways you have supported me. And to my father, former English teacher and enthusiastic editor of my drafts: You continue to teach me every day how to be a better writer and, more importantly, how to be a better person.

One of the greatest experiences in writing this book was the opportunity I had to talk with so many inspiring educators and university administrators across higher education. As I conducted interviews, discussed pedagogy, and bounced ideas for innovation off of these folks, I was constantly impressed with their insights, their ingenuity, and their determination. I would particularly like to thank the many colleagues who assisted with this project through agreeing to be interviewed, including Andy Mink, Rashmi Assudani, Gabriela Weaver, Jake Mazulewicz, Mike Deibel, Monica Rico, Michael Birkel, Jen Ostergren, the students at Brigham Young University, and Peter Felton. I would also like to express my gratitude to my many mentors and colleagues who have inspired me along the way, including Doug Bennett, Mark Burstein, Len Clark, Karlyn Crowley, David Dawson, Lynn Morton, Heather Pleasants, and all the 2019–20 American Council on Education (ACE) Fellows. There are also many, many more teachers and facilitators I have worked with over the years—too many to acknowledge here. But each encounter and interaction has had an influence on me and on this book.

Finally, I would also like to thank the editorial staff at Routledge Press for taking such good care of me and this book project—in particular Heather Jarrow, who capably managed me and this project from start to finish.

REFERENCES

Jay, M. (2005). *Songs of experience: Modern American and European variations on a universal theme.* Berkeley, CA: University of California Press.

Part One
Our Uncertain World

Chapter 1

Introduction

On a cold January day in 2001, I officially began my journey as a college professor. I was assigned to a lecture hall for a class of approximately 50 undergraduates who had signed up for EDUC 120 "Foundations of Education"—a classic survey course for students interested in teaching and a possible career in education. In the fall, I had been given the syllabus for the course from the previous professor, and I dutifully went about organizing the material for the semester. Having just completed graduate school the year before, I decided to add to his reading list (which I thought was a bit out of date). I also decided to add several new units to the course to make it "mine," distinct from previous offerings. The previous instructor was a seasoned full professor at my institution with more than a few miles on the odometer and enough classroom (and life) experience to put me in my place. But, as I sat in his rather musty old office amid all the papers and books stacked everywhere the eye could see, proposing my grand plans for a redesigned course, he wisely recognized youthful hubris when he saw it, listened attentively, and then offered the requisite amount of encouragement and sent me on my way. There is an old saying in wilderness guide circles: "You gotta go to know." I think, in that moment, my colleague was probably thinking something like that in his head as he listened to an overly confident and underprepared junior faculty member about to wander into his first class.

The fact is, very few of us go through graduate school and the rigorous process of attaining a terminal degree and exit prepared to teach. Centers for teaching and learning are increasingly commonplace on larger campuses, but, even with the additional resources and support, the vast majority of us who become teachers have little formal training and experience to draw from. That was certainly the case for me. As I imagined my first class, I thought back to the classes I loved as an undergraduate and graduate student. I conjured fantastical images of me, Dr. Inspiration, presiding over a room filled with students eager to learn. I also thought back to classes that I didn't like and made plans to make *my* classroom much more engaging. And fun. With snacks! We teach as we are taught, and so it was with me that first semester.

But a funny thing happened on the way through that first, cold winter in Indiana. The students that I prepared for were not the students I got. The syllabus and classes I designed did not immediately conjure a lecture hall filled with engaged undergraduates. One day, after two weeks of awkward and educationally dubious classes, I trudged back to my office feeling thoroughly defeated. As I sat there, wondering whether I was really cut out to be a professor, there was a tentative knock on the door. "Excuse me, Jay? I'm wondering if you have a second to talk about class?" One of my students, using the familiar first name of professors common in Quaker schools, poked her head in. I perked up. Ah ha! Here we go! My first office visit. I spun around, hoping to clarify for her the complex social theory of John Dewey we just went over in class. This was more like it! "Um," she began, "as a senior, I've had the chance to take lots of classes and different professors and I'm just wondering if you might want to consider sitting in on Gordon's class to see how he leads better class discussions?" Gordon was Gordon Thompson, a full professor of English who, by all accounts, was a pedagogical genius in a tweed jacket. Past and present students would speak of Gordon's classes as akin to a spiritual experience where they bared their souls, became lifelong friends, and forever changed the way they thought about everything. This was not what I had wanted to hear. "Gordon Thompson?" I said rather defensively. "He's been teaching for, like 25 years. I doubt I can be like Gordon." "Well," she said, as she picked up her things and headed for the door, "you have to start somewhere."

Teaching is risky. When we enter into the ritualistic space of the classroom, we bring with us practices, assumptions, stereotypes, and misconceptions about the art and the science of learning. Teachers, throughout the ages, are assumed to "know things." A student asks a question and we answer it. We aren't supposed to respond with something like, "I don't know that." Once, early on in my career, I was giving a lecture on *Brown v. Board of Education* and the early attempts at desegregating schools in the United States. A student raised his hand and asked, "Where did the phrase 'Jim Crow laws' come from?" I had not expected this question. Worse, I did not know the answer. Fifty blank faces stared at me out of the silence. My mind raced in that teacher-brain sort of way, furiously multitasking the problem at hand. One part of my brain was running back through everything I'd learned about the civil rights era and desegregation in an attempt to resurrect this factoid from the recesses of my memory. The other part of my brain was contingency planning. What else can I say besides, "I don't know?" Mind you, this was pre-Google, when a basic question like that could instantly deliver a Wikipedia answer. In those days, we teachers were Alexa, Siri, and Hey Google wrapped into one. *We* were the smart device. In the end, I made some lame attempt at an answer before surrendering and just saying that I didn't know, but that I would find out and come back next time with the answer. I felt so . . . *incompetent*. For years I would think back on this in my moments of insecurity and replay it over and over in my head.

INTRODUCTION

We call it the "imposter syndrome" when we don't feel as though we deserve to be in a given position. Teachers, and professors in particular, suffer from imposter syndrome. This can be especially true for historically underrepresented faculty including women, first generation, and teachers of color. Tradition says we are expected to *know* the answers. We are the content-level experts. It is our job. So, every time we walk into that classroom, we take a risk. In the imposter syndrome kind of way, we risk being "found out." That, in fact, we don't know what we should know or claim to know. Therese Huston, in her wonderful book, *Teaching What You Don't Know*, argues that the "teaching as telling" mode sets us up for this fear of being found out as an imposter.

> Perhaps therein lies the true imposter syndrome. It's not just that I'm pretending to be a medical anthropologist when I'm not, or that I'm feigning expertise as a nuclear engineer when I'm so clearly not. What's bothering me is that at some core level, I'm also an imposter as a teacher. If I believe that teaching is about telling, and I'm teaching material that I don't know very well, I can't tell you very much.
>
> (Huston, 2009, p. 42)

Huston's book is all about trying out perhaps the riskiest thing of all—teaching something you yourself don't know. In essence, purposefully choosing to be a content novice. Teaching what you don't know brings into the harsh sunlight our fundamental assumptions about what it means to be a teacher. If we are no longer the content-level expert, what are we? Who are we? One of the key takeaways from her book, to me, is this: "it's the pretending that gets you into trouble" (Ibid., p. 39). Once we move off the teacher as expert and the teaching as telling paradigm, we have to embrace something we usually try to avoid in teaching: vulnerability. One of the strange side effects of our perception of risk in teaching is a tendency to put up barriers and façades to protect ourselves from getting hurt. Parker Palmer writes, in *The Courage to Teach*, about the walls we can put up to mitigate the risks. "To reduce our vulnerability, we disconnect from students, from subjects, and even from ourselves. We build a wall between our inner truth and outer performance and we play-act the teacher's part" (Palmer, 2009, p. 17). Whether we are teaching something we are confident in or teaching new material, many of us can admit to this fear of being found out or of being an imposter and to feeling like we are playing the role of what we think a teacher should be even if it isn't us. Grappling with this is a fundamental part of risky teaching. Saying "I don't know" is risky and feels vulnerable. And this can be much more challenging for women and for our faculty of color as they navigate the gender and racial dynamics of the classroom and college environment. Being willing to be vulnerable in the classroom can be a privileged position.

Another teaching risk is simply being wrong. Perhaps the only thing worse than not knowing the answer is to be *corrected* by a student. Once, while leading an off-campus study semester in environmental studies in New Zealand, I confidently declared that the plant we were looking at was a Hebe. "No, it's not," said one of my students who happened to be majoring in biology and was on top of her plant identification, "it's a Coprosma." I looked at her and looked back at the plant, checked the guidebook, and admitted my failings. Ouch. As Palmer notes, teaching is a type of performance. We perform expertise in front of our students (while they perform learning in front of us). Like acting, this performance can be nerve-racking. As in a stage show, we have an audience. But rather than having to perform in front of an audience that might include perhaps one or two (professional) critics, for us it seems as though the entire class is writing a review for the local entertainment section of the news. And, in fact, sometimes they do—it's called a course evaluation. Unlike most other stage productions, our audience doesn't necessarily want to be there and may feel hard done by as they consider the cost of that very expensive ticket they hold in their hand to participate in a performance the relevance of which they often question. If we forget our lines (a common teacher nightmare), we face derision and ridicule. Actors may tremble at the thought of the review in the arts section of the local news; we teachers open our course evaluations with shaking hands and learn to avoid spending time on Rate My Professor and other such sites.

However, beyond knowing, not knowing, or getting it wrong, there is another risk we take as teachers. Knowing a lot and getting the content right (most of the time) are perhaps a necessary but insufficient account of the educational endeavor. We also must know how to teach it to others. And this is also a risk—a *pedagogical* risk. When we consider the activities, ideas, or strategies to teach content, we are like (to use another stage analogy) the jazz band heading into improvisation. The structure may be known ahead of time (the sheet music in jazz and the lesson plan in teaching), but how we riff off of that structure in concert with others and create something memorable, lasting, and even transformative is the art form of both jazz and teaching. Do it poorly as a jazz musician and patrons head for the exits. And there are no do-overs in the moment. If you mess up, you just have to play through it.

One semester, I decided to teach a small, faculty-student research experience focused on creating a climate action plan for the college to lower our greenhouse gas footprint. "How hard could it be?" I thought at the time. I get my students to research various alternative energy options for the campus, and we present our findings to the community at the end of the semester. I had never led a faculty-student research group before, and, once again, I imagined how the semester would go. My small band of acolytes and I would dive into the research and data, exploring the topic in depth and spending hours (as I did in graduate school) thinking about the topic from every which way. This did not happen. It turned out, the students had *other* classes in addition to this research group. And, they weren't exactly clear on how to *do* research. For some strange reason, they expected me to teach them. I know how to do research. But I had never really considered how to teach someone else how to do research. And this was a fatal disconnect. I gave the students too little structure and far too much independence. As I sat in the back of the lecture hall watching my acolytes present their fabulously mediocre final research papers on climate action planning, I realized, much too late, my mistake. I hadn't *taught* them what they needed to know. And here they were, flailing in front of an audience of their peers (and other faculty), and it was my fault. I vowed from that point forward that I would never again assume that teaching *anything* would be easy.

Learning is also risky. As teachers, we can sometimes forget what it feels like to learn something new. The book, lab, or activity we are introducing in class is often one we have read or completed before, and we have usually spent time organizing and preparing the content before our students arrive. But for students, this is the first time. Sometimes we teachers fail at the empathy game with our students. However, we can be quickly reminded of what learning feels like and the risks associated with it when we, as faculty, are exposed to something new and novel. As I write this, faculty all over this country and the world have been teaching in the midst of the Covid-19 global pandemic and through an academic year like no other. Faculty who just six months ago knew nothing about "remote learning" have had to get up to speed on learning management systems, Zoom, Google Meets, and how to create interactive online classes. Suddenly, professors who are used to "professing" must now sit back and learn. And make mistakes. And perhaps even look foolish in front of their peers (and their students) as they struggle to figure out how to make their damn camera and microphone work. In this new world, our students are actually quite a bit more comfortable than we are. Learning is often risky, and sometimes, in the moment, it doesn't always feel great. One of the possible silver linings of this terrible pandemic is that faculty are experiencing learning in brand new ways and, maybe, enhancing their ability to empathize with their students as a result. Teaching and learning go hand in hand, and *both* are risky endeavors. As our students learn, they are taking countless risks. I would say that learning is at its most powerful and most transformative in the presence of risk. And in order for students to take risks and learn, we as faculty have to take risks in teaching. In many ways, you cannot have risky learning without risky teaching.

THE HAZARDS OF RISK

This is a book about risk and uncertainty in teaching and learning. But, before we consider issues of methodology and how to work best with risk and uncertainty in and out of the classroom, it would be worth a little more time thinking about risk and uncertainty—how we define these terms and what they come to signify in our work in colleges and universities. As a humanist, I am inclined to explore the conceptual framework of the work first, before we dig into the methodological details. How do we define risk? What is the etymology of the word? What are the multiple meanings of uncertainty?

Our common understanding of risk is negative. During your pre-tenure career, a colleague might say, "I wouldn't do that—it's not worth the risk." Or, in our current Covid-19 context, we might think about the risks associated with reopening schools. We risk illness or even death among our students, our faculty, and our staff. As a result of this negative frame, we seek to avoid risks in a variety of contexts. We decide to go all online rather than have classes in person. We move our investments into less risky portfolios as we get older. We choose to make a new policy on campus prohibiting something or another due to risk management. In each of these cases, taking a risk is viewed as an inherently negative thing. Risk entails the possibility of loss or injury. There are good reasons we humans seek to avoid such things.

And, there are good reasons to avoid risk in higher education. Pre-tenure faculty are almost universally advised to avoid taking risks before they go up for review. They are told to keep quiet, don't make a fuss, and work on publications and (perhaps) teaching. Student life personnel spend a lot of time educating students about "risky behaviors" to ensure a campus climate that is as safe as we can make it for student living and learning. And, at the broadest possible level, institutions of higher learning also tend to avoid risks. During one strategic planning period at my former institution, we were discussing whether or not to try a bold new initiative that some faculty thought promising in faculty meeting. A seasoned professor of history got to his feet and said, "While we must always aim to be *distinctive*, we must also avoid looking *peculiar*." In his cautionary remarks, this faculty member was describing a fear shared in most institutions of higher education. While we want to innovate and be known for this or that creative program or initiative, we most decidedly do *not* want to be considered weird. Academic reputation matters a lot. This can lead to a risk-averse organizational culture and even, one could argue, a sector-wide aversion to risk.

For a brief period of time in the mid-to-late 2000s, a group of college presidents in the United States attempted to challenge the power and the influence of the *US News and World Report* (*USNWR*) rankings by pulling out of the survey and refusing to participate in the reputational ranking scores—something most would admit is hardly a scientific way of measuring the quality of a school. The move gained some press and even a small amount of traction, including a story in *The Chronicle of Higher Education*.[1] This was an admittedly risky thing to do. Back then, and even more so today, the annual *USNWR* rankings could make or break a president, chief enrollment officer, and even an institution. Boards fret over drops in rankings. Prospective students and families can choose or dismiss a school outright based on the magazine's rankings. Pulling out of the survey can have real costs—both reputationally and financially. In hindsight, while the effort was noble and raised much-needed criticism of the *USNWR* methodology, the risk proved too great. Only a handful of schools ended up refusing to participate and, in the end, might have paid a price with a drop in the ranking system, proving that being the first to do something can be perilous.

RISK AND OPPORTUNITY

But there are other ways we can define and view risk. Entrepreneurs often talk about the connections between risk and opportunity. One of my favorite axioms is "A ship is safe in the harbor but that is not what ships are made for." Risk isn't always something to be avoided. In fact, life would be a terribly boring place without a degree of risk. Some of the best moments of my life came from taking a deliberate risk—asking my wife to marry me, deciding to drop out of graduate school, and hauling my family (including a 1- and a 3-year-old) across the world to do a semester study abroad in New Zealand. I wasn't entirely sure how any of those decisions would go, and they all involved the possibility of peril at some level (try being stuck on a plane for 15 hours with a 1-year-old). But they also offered up opportunity. Wikipedia notes a secondary definition of risk following the more typical (and negative) frame about perils and hazards: "Risk can also be defined as the intentional interaction with uncertainty. Uncertainty is a potential, unpredictable, and uncontrollable outcome; risk is an aspect of action taken in spite of uncertainty." Here, risk isn't seen as merely a negative. It brings in our other term to explore—*uncertainty*. Uncertainty, like risk, can have both negative and positive connotations. In our present moment, the uncertainty of the global pandemic is viewed almost entirely negatively. We do not like the ambiguity, the unknown, and the feeling of being out of control as we watch this virus move among us and wreak economic and social havoc. We don't know where it is at any given time, we don't know how long it will be here, and we don't know what will happen to us if we are exposed. And, if you are like me, we are all growing *very* tired of phrases like, "in these uncertain times." Right now, we all have uncertainty fatigue.

But, whether or not we are enjoying this particular bout with uncertainty, it is also true that uncertainty has positive, creative qualities as well. There are ways to think about risk and uncertainty that open up the conversation beyond the more constraining definition of risk as a form of peril or loss. Uncertainty is simply a fact of life. It cannot be avoided. While we can sometimes dislike uncertainty, we also often purposefully seek it out. Consider something as simple as attending a movie or a live sporting event (whenever we have the opportunity to do that again). In most such cases, part of the entertainment value of going is that you *don't know in advance what the outcome will be*. That is what makes it engaging. In fact, our modern culture has a phrase we use to attempt to ensure the value of such experiences: "spoiler alerts." Take away the uncertainty and you spoil the fun.

One summer day I knew I would have to miss a big soccer match coming up in the World Cup later that afternoon, so I recorded it. I carefully avoided all news and social media throughout the day so I could return home that night to watch the game in its entirety. As I packed up my things to leave the office that afternoon, a colleague popped in and said excitedly, "Can you believe how badly Germany beat Brazil?!" I stared at him like he'd just shot my dog. He apologized profusely, but there is simply no taking back a spoiler. Now that I knew the outcome, it was far less interesting. I did wind up watching the match later that night, but without any of the excitement, engagement, and anticipation of being in the moment of an unknown outcome.

There are small "u" uncertainties, such as not knowing when the train will actually get here or how your lunch will taste when you try out the new food truck. Then there are big "U" uncertainties like tenure, whether you'll get pregnant, or whether a cancer diagnosis will be terminal. Neuroscience tells us that uncertainty can generate different responses in the brain. The right amount of perceived uncertainty can be stimulating and engaging, as in attending that sporting event, watching a thriller, or reading a page-turner. Yet, too much uncertainty can be debilitating, even traumatic. A child who doesn't know where her next meal is coming from is not reveling in uncertainty. It is, in the end, a privilege to celebrate uncertainty in one's life. When your basic needs are met, you can then allow other aspects of your life to be purposefully out of control and enjoy that. For example, if I already have a good job, one that pays well and that I enjoy, *and* I am contacted by a headhunter who wants to recruit me to another institution, I can enjoy that process of uncertainty. Do I stay? Do I go? But this obviously changes if I am unemployed, have loads of student debt, and am trying to land *any* kind of teaching job in higher education. That uncertainty has a different weight and effect. We are experiencing this kind of uncertainty now as we live through the pandemic. *Too much* is uncertain.

So, risk is a weighted term—both individually and culturally. Depending upon the conditions and context, it can denote something negative or something positive. We often attempt to avoid it, or seek to manage it, or hedge against it, but we are also drawn toward it. Often, the same set of circumstances can be seen both ways—as negatively perilous *and* positively uncertain and filled with potential opportunity, depending on the individual and the context. Recently, my wife and I were caught in a serious thunderstorm driving through the mountains in Kentucky. It was one of those storms where the windshield wipers were going as fast as they could go and doing very little to create a clear view. It was fascinating to watch the responses from the drivers around us. Here we all were, with little visibility, driving a car (or truck) 60–80 miles per hour down a mountain highway. Some people decided to pull over and wait the storm out. Some, like us, decided to put our hazard lights on, slow down, and move over into the right lane. A few daring (or stupid) folks decided to just proceed as if nothing had changed and continued their current speed. While the risk was objective (rain, lack of visibility, slick roads), the perception of that risk was subjective.

RISKY TEACHING AND LEARNING

The point is that one person's thrilling engagement with risk and uncertainty can be another person's worst nightmare. There is a subjective quality to the ways in which we perceive risk and uncertainty. A shy student in class who is considering taking a risk and speaking is going through the same things, physiologically, as another person who may be 1,000 feet up a sheer rock face: elevated heart rate, shallow breathing, sweaty palms, and a dry mouth. A pre-tenure faculty member teaching a course for the first time may be (but not always) less willing to take risks and experiment pedagogically than the tenured professor who has been around the block a few times. There are real and objective reasons why students and faculty may want to avoid risk. But I am not certain that explains the whole of it. Even given objective constraints, there are ways we can see and work with risk in and out of our classrooms that present opportunities for us *and for our students*, not just peril.

Allowing that the word risk is complex and comes with both negative and positive connotations, as well as objective and subjective attributes,[1] here is the way I will frame and define "risky teaching": **Risky teaching is the deliberate and purposeful incorporation of productive uncertainty in learning situations**. That uncertainty can be student-centered, teacher-centered, or both. Importantly, productive uncertainty is designed as a means to some educational end (not as an end in itself). Not all uncertainty is productive, and, in an educational sense, we want to use uncertainty to reach clearly defined goals and objectives. That is what I mean by productive uncertainty. Risky teaching is not a method, per se, though there are a host of methods that can be employed to create productive states of uncertainty. It is more an orientation to the teaching and learning enterprise—a mode of being rather than a technique to be used in isolation. In this sense, and as we will discuss in more detail in Chapter 4 on risk and the teacher, it can be viewed as an "infinite game" (Carse, 2011)—something to embody and constantly work on.

So, this is a book about teaching and learning through risk and productive uncertainty in higher education. It is a book for faculty, instructors, and staff in higher education who want to experiment with different forms of learning both in and out of the classroom. As I will discuss in the next chapter, it is also a book that I believe is particularly relevant in our current situation. We, and our students, are living through turbulent and uncertain times. While there are elements within higher education that should *not* necessarily be responsive to the immediate issues and trends of the day, there is also an ethical obligation for colleges and universities to speak to the concerns of our students and society. How can we, as teachers, model being more comfortable with uncertainty, ambiguity, and even adversity? How can we help our students do likewise? Such forms of teaching and learning can also lead to better learning outcomes (more on that later).

My writing this book is another form of risk-taking. If there is one thing I have learned in 25 years of working with students and faculty in higher education, declaring oneself an expert on teaching is the surest way to ruin. Good faculty development follows our models of good pedagogy. "Less sage on the stage and more guide on the side," as they say. A former student shared a meme with me recently: "A good teacher shows you where to look but not what to see." In this sense, I hope this book allows the reader to have a look at the roles of risk and uncertainty in teaching and learning. I also hope that in looking, you may find useful tools, principles, models, or examples for your own practice. But I don't expect you to see exactly what I see or teach exactly the way I teach. Teaching is such a deeply personal act. There are certainly evidence-based practices that have been shown to increase engagement and learning, and we will explore many of those throughout this book. But those practices are like the squares of a quilt. They must be sewn together in a meaningful pattern of the individual's choosing. Every quilt will be different, shaped by the background, life experiences, and personality of the instructor.

I have been teaching in higher education for over 20 years, mostly at small, liberal arts colleges but with important early experiences at larger public universities in graduate school as a teaching assistant and instructor. In the classroom, I have experimented with a range of methods from active and game-based learning to project-based learning. Out of the classroom, I have designed service learning and community-engaged research projects and have led a number of off-campus study experiences—from several weeks to full semester study abroad programs. I've also spent time, as a younger professional, as an outdoor guide and instructor—taking students and trainees into remote wilderness environments backpacking, climbing, and canoeing. The lessons I learned about risk and uncertainty in these contexts have stayed with me to this day. I have taught through uncertainty in a variety of ways over the years, and I will share what I have learned. Almost everything I will introduce and discuss in this book I have experienced as a teacher and as a learner. Many of the methods articulated in this book come from others. I am grateful to have had mentors, guides, and wise souls throughout my career who have greatly influenced my teaching. The ideas expressed here represent a bricolage of experiences, successes, failures, and lessons learned with and from others.

As I have grown in my career, I have also had the opportunity to visit a variety of institutions—big and small, public and private—and to work with other faculty on these ideas. Through those interactions, I have seen what has resonated and what has worked for faculty across a range of institutional contexts. This has helped me ground truth and test my own sense of what works with what I have learned from others. In researching this book, I also spent time interviewing a variety of teachers and leaders in higher education—from small schools to large public institutions—to expand my own understanding of risky teaching and learning. I will share their stories and perspectives along the way too.

CONCLUSION

I recently heard from a former student who had taken a class of mine ("Pedagogies of Place") several years ago and is now working out in the world. She wrote,

> I wanted to reach out to you, first of all, to say thank you. My time at Earlham was defined by the experiences and learning opportunities provided to me by teachers like you. I have been working for an environmental education foundation for the past five years, designing and teaching place-based curriculum, both as a teacher, and now as a Camp Director. It is in large part due to Pedagogies of Place, with you, that I found myself in this place, so thank you!

We teachers love to get messages like this, and I am sure, if you are reading this and are a teacher, you have received your fair share. It reminds us of why we do what we do. It gets us through the endless meetings, grading, and "administrivia" of college professorship. We are not, after all, in the business of producing widgets. And, perhaps more radically, *we are not in the business of teaching*. We are first and foremost in the business of *student learning*. But beyond that, I firmly believe that our deepest calling, as educators, is the care and nurturing of the human soul. The outcome we are after, after we strip off all the superficialities and the technocratic learning goals and objectives, is for our students to flourish in society. When we hear from students who remember us and who recall how a class influenced who they have become, it is deeply humbling and gratifying.

But, because this is a book about risky teaching and learning, it is important for me to note that this student and the outcomes she describes came from my taking a risk. In 2008, I had just returned from leading a semester study abroad program in New Zealand and was working on a new course for our environmental studies majors. It was a course aimed at introducing students to the concept of place in environmental thought. As I thought through how I wanted to design the syllabus, I kept going back to my experiences with students in New Zealand. One memory, in particular, stayed with me. Early on in the program, we experienced a Treaty workshop—a standard program in New Zealand that is similar to, but not quite the same as, an anti-racist workshop in the United States. As part of the workshop, the facilitators divided us into geographic groupings based on our hometown locations (Northeast, Midwest, South, West, etc.) and asked us to talk with each other about what we knew of the Native American groups that existed in those areas—either historically or in the present day. To our shame, we didn't know a lot. When the facilitators brought us back together and we revealed our limited knowledge, they gave us a challenge: "You traveled all the way around the world to learn about Māori culture and New Zealand history. When you leave, we ask you to be as motivated to learn about your own."

As I stared at my computer screen trying to design the course, I thought about how engaged my students were in New Zealand and how naturally curious they were about the content. How could I orchestrate that same level of engagement back at Earlham? Was it even possible? That simple question led me to my risky teaching moment: What if I designed the class in a way that mimicked an off-campus study experience? Of course, this was impossible. The off-campus study semester we experienced was immersive—meaning that students took all four classes together as a cohort with my wife and me serving as co-leaders. This allowed us to orchestrate field trips, longer classes, and experiential components in a way that would be logistically impossible back home in a traditional 15-week semester. Plus, New Zealand was, well, *New Zealand*. It was easy for students to get engaged. Richmond, Indiana, is not New Zealand. But the risky proposition of replicating the *feel* of that semester stayed with me and I began to dream.

In the end, and as I discuss in more detail in Chapter 4, I designed a course that still fit within the traditional 15-week semester structure but included new immersive and experiential components woven in. I wanted a course that could, in some small way, replicate the "strange lands" curiosity of that New Zealand semester. And one that was attentive to place and history in the ways our Treaty workshop facilitators challenged us to be. I had no idea how it would go. The student who emailed me experienced the *third* iteration of that course. There were bumps and bruises along the way as I developed that course, but I was willing to take that risk and it remains one of my favorites. And, perhaps more importantly, that class is consistently one former students talk about when I hear from them.

Risky teaching and learning are not easy. By definition, no type of risk is. And it is important to note that we should not strive to live in a perpetual state of risk-taking. We need our moments and days of comfort, safety, and routine. But the opportunities that exist for us, and for our students, to step outside our comfort zones and stretch are so often worth it. As Pema Chodron writes in *When Things Fall Apart*,

> The trick is to keep on exploring and not bail out, even when we find something is not what we thought. That's what we're going to discover again and again and again. Nothing is what we thought. I can say that with great confidence.... These are words that point to what life really is when we let things fall apart and let ourselves be nailed to the present moment.
>
> (2005, p. 6)

Of the risks I have taken in my life that were good ones and for good reasons, I have never regretted any of them—even though some were abject failures. It is, after all, how we grow. And growth, development, maturation, and transformation—these are the deeper aims and values of higher education. And of that, I am certain.

NOTE

1. See "Annapolis Group Challenges 'US News' Rankings." Retrieved from: www.chronicle.com/article/Annapolis-Group-Challenges/13200

REFERENCES

Carse, J. (2011). *Finite and infinite games*. New York: Simon and Schuster.

Chodron, P. (2005). *When things fall apart*. Berkeley, CA: Shambhala Publications.

Huston, T. (2009). *Teaching what you don't know*. Boston, MA: Harvard University Press.

Palmer, P. J. (2009). *The courage to teach*. New York: John Wiley & Sons.

Risk. (n.d.). In *Wikipedia*. Retrieved February 12, 2021, from: https://en.m.wikipedia.org/wiki/Risk

Chapter 2

Uncertainty in Higher Education

INTRODUCTION

Early in my teaching career, I led a summer, outdoor, pre-orientation backpacking program in Utah with ten incoming first-year students and two older student leaders. It was a wonderful experience filled with significant learning—both for the students and for me. One of the things you have to pick up fairly quickly when you are out in wilderness areas where cell phones and Google maps don't work is how to orient and read a paper map. The maps you take into places like this are 7.5-minute US Geological Survey "quad" maps that have topographic lines and show key features like rivers, peaks, and lakes. They are quite handy and accurate—if you know how to use them. One of the activities we do toward the conclusion of the program is a graduation exercise of sorts. We tell the students it is their turn to lead, and the instructors (myself and the two older students) drop back and intervene only if there is a safety problem. During one of those student-led days, the first-year students headed off confidently down the trail without referencing the map much. Two hours later, they came to a spot where the trail was no longer discernible. In this part of the Uinta Mountains of Utah, the trails sometimes disappear once you get above the tree line. If you have your maps and know how to orient them correctly, this is usually just a minor challenge. A quick check of the map and your compass and you know where you need to go. In this case, however, the students were still learning, and they had made the cardinal error of not referencing their location along the way as they hiked—leaving them with a lot of guesswork once they stopped and actually tried to orient themselves.

After a good long look at the map and some heated conversation among themselves, the group came to a consensus as to which way they ought to go and off they went—in the exact opposite direction of where they should be going. As the instructor team, we exchanged glances that communicated, "how long should we let them do this?" We silently trailed behind them as they headed off down a ridge in search of a trail they were sure would intersect their path in the next mile. After

30 minutes of hiking, when that trail did not materialize, the students stopped again to reconsider. Some thought they should keep heading down slope. Others thought they should turn around. The atmosphere was tense. One of the things that happens when you find yourself "temporarily misplaced" in the outdoors is the tendency for the mind to play tricks. Looking at the map and looking at the terrain, you can "bend the map" to a preconceived notion of where you *want* to be, not necessarily where you are. You "bend" that stream on the map to be the river you see in front of you. Or that hill on the map to be the 10,000-foot peak in the distance. The mind doesn't like paradox or dissonance for long—it seeks resolution. In this instance, the students were "bending the map" in the hopes of discovering where they were. They turned the map this way and that, trying to orient it to the terrain they were experiencing. After debating their location for a time, they finally agreed on the proper orientation and figured out (approximately) where they were and where they needed to go. The 30 minutes of downslope, off-trail hiking turned into an hour of uphill slogging to wind up right back where they started. Lesson learned.

Metaphorically, I think we orient ourselves to "maps" in lots of ways. These are usually cognitive maps or frames of reference born from experience. When we do so, we are trying to understand where we are and where we need to go based upon some context or landscape that we are moving through. A moment of uncertainty arises, however, when we realize that the "map is not the territory" so to speak. Suddenly, we look at the map with fresh eyes. Is it oriented correctly? Have we made assumptions about where we are? We often try to bend the map (without reorienting it) in the hope that it will still be useful in the new, unfamiliar context. Sometimes, we may even discover that we have been looking at the wrong map all along.

In this particular moment, I think the world in general and higher education specifically are undergoing a reorientation of our maps. When this occurs, it can be disorienting. Where are we? How did we get here? Which way are we supposed to go? It is a kind of uncertainty that can leave us unclear, tentative, and anxious. As Margaret Wheatley noted in her work *Turning To One Another: Simple Conversations to Restore Hope in the Future*,

> We weren't trained to admit we don't know. Most of us were taught to sound certain and confident, to state our opinion as if it were true. We haven't been rewarded for being confused. Or for asking more questions rather than giving quick answers.
>
> But the world now is quite perplexing. We no longer live in those sweet, slow days when life felt predictable, when we actually knew what to do next. We live in a complex world, we often don't know what's going on, and we won't be able to understand its complexity unless we spend more time in not knowing.

> It is very difficult to give up our certainties—our positions, our beliefs, our explanations. These help define us; they lie at the heart of our personal identity. Yet I believe we will succeed in changing this world only if we can think and work together in new ways.
>
> (2002, p. 42)

It can be difficult indeed to let go of our certainties. Eventually, as with my students in the Uinta Wilderness area of Utah, reality comes crashing back in. We realize that learning online requires a different approach to content and engagement. Recording lectures and posting them to a learning management system is not really teaching—it is bending the map. While I suppose every person believes at some level that the era they are living through is the most important or consequential, I think there is a real argument to be made that, in terms of higher education, the phase we are moving through now, in the first two decades of the 21st century, is Copernican in its scale and scope. Many have referred to this era as the "Great Disruption" to signal the ways that social, economic, technological, and demographic forces are fundamentally reshaping higher education. And this was *before* Covid-19. Now, higher education is experiencing an almost unimaginable perfect storm of challenges as the global pandemic impacts nearly every facet of the organization and operation of colleges and universities. Students and families have less income due to the economic downturn, public funding is stretched to the limit as states struggle to meet their responsibilities, and institutions have been hit with a significant reduction in revenue from a loss of room and board fees and drops in overall enrollment.

As if these challenges weren't enough, the summer of 2020 in the United States brought racial justice to the forefront as the country faced the grim realities of the deaths of George Floyd and Breanna Taylor and the systemic racism that we have ignored for far too long. Students, faculty, and alumni rallied to call colleges and universities to account for their failure to address the concerns and lived experiences of Black, Indigenous, and people of color on our campuses. I sat on a cabinet and experienced the justifiable anger and frustration of students and faculty. It was a moment to reorient our maps. As Wheatley (2002) suggests, we had "to give up our certainties—our positions, our beliefs, our explanations" and recognize that we really did not know. It was not a time to issue grand pronouncements of empathy and support. It was a time to listen, to learn, and to consult. The resulting demands issued by students and the Black Lives Matter (BLM) movement to address racial injustice represent an opportunity to reorient our maps. Rather than attempt to bend the map to our current way of seeing the world, it is clear that we need to wrestle with the complexity, the uncertainty, and the discomfort that come when the former map is no longer useful. But doing so may leave us, like those students in the Uinta Wilderness, wandering well off the trail. The social, economic, technological, and demographic changes and challenges we are experiencing provide the backdrop for why risk and uncertainty are the new normal for the sector. There are also many good reasons for wanting all the risk and uncertainty to go away. A former colleague of mine joked, "Can we have a disruption from all the disruption, please?" It is psychically difficult to manage this much uncertainty for long, and we hope that, at least with the global pandemic, we achieve herd immunity and develop a universally effective and available vaccine soon. We shouldn't have to risk our bodies and our lives—the lives and health of our children, our teachers, our essential workers, and our most vulnerable in society. However, even when we do find our way into a future where Covid-19 is manageable, when we come to grips with our past and present racial injustice, and when we can *all* feel a little safer, uncertainty and risk will still be there. The terrain in front of us will have forever changed. Our old maps will no longer be useful. The question is this: Given the disruptions, how do we reorient our maps? As Wheatley (2002) writes, "I believe we will succeed in changing this world only if we can think and work together in new ways." This work requires us to work *with* uncertainty and to be willing to take risks. How we do that with our students will be the subject of the subsequent chapters in this book. But to start, it is worth exploring briefly the social, economic, technological, and demographic contours of our newly reoriented map in higher education.

THE ECONOMIC REORIENTATION

On March 16, 2008, the brokerage firm Bear Stearns collapsed, sending shock waves throughout the global financial world. While economists now believe the so-called Great Recession began in late 2007, it was the shocking and sudden failure of Bear Stearns that signaled something was very wrong in the global economy. In the following months, a stunning series of bankruptcies followed, while Freddie Mac and Fannie Mae, the two companies that guarantee the majority of mortgages in the United States, went into receivership with the US Treasury. By March of 2009, the US stock market had reached its nadir—losing more than 50 percent of its prerecession value from 2007. It was only later, after the dust had settled, that reports trickled out about how close the United States and the rest of the world had come to a global economic catastrophe.

    I remember, as a faculty member, watching all of this happen back in 2008 with a combination of morbid fascination and real fear. My retirement savings took a significant hit, and so did the endowment of my college. One study found that universities lost, on average, 23 percent of their endowments in late 2008 (Zezima, 2009; Commonfund Institute, 2009). "Would this necessitate cuts?" I thought. What impact would this have on our operating budget? At the time, I didn't fully grasp the impact this economic downturn would have not just on my own institution but the entire sector. I thought, at worst, institutions like mine would have to adjust to leaner operating budgets for a period of time. This was, in fact, what happened at my college—we cut back on spending and hiring. But what I didn't fully understand back in 2008 was the *generational* impact of the Great Recession and the perception of the value of a higher education degree. Millennials were coming of age during this time period, and the recession had a lasting impact on their attitudes about spending and finance. As Griswold (2014) noted, "Millennials are the most financially conservative generation to come around since the Great Depression."

Beyond millennials, the Great Recession seems to have served as a giant, global "reset" button in terms of the public perception of higher education. Prior to 2008, while there were some concerns about college costs, about the value of the liberal arts, and the extent to which a degree guaranteed a "return on investment," these issues did not dominate the larger public discussion and perception of the purposes and aims of college. But the Great Recession took these concerns and amplified them. I graduated from college in 1992 in the midst of a recession, and while finding gainful employment was the dominant issue of the day, student debt and affordability issues were barely acknowledged. Now, in 2020, student debt is the second highest consumer debt category eclipsing credit card debt and second only to home mortgages, totaling $1.56 trillion (Friedman, 2019). At least two presidential candidates in the 2020 election in the United States made free college a central plank in their policy platforms.

These forces have reshaped family perceptions of higher education. The old economic value proposition (it still holds true, by the way) was that the cost and the potential debt incurred for an undergraduate degree were worth the investment given the return of future earnings. However, since the Great Recession, perceptions of this value appear to have changed. According to Brandon Busteed, President of Kaplan University Partners and former Executive Director of Education and Workforce Development for Gallup,

> When asked about a potential new pathway for their children to get a college degree, 74% of all parents of K–12 students would consider a route where their child would be hired directly out of high school by an employer that offers a college degree while working. . . . Remarkably, there are no meaningful differences in support for this new pathway by the parent's education level, race, income or political affiliation giving the concept broad appeal across the board. And parents not only see this path as a much more affordable route through college, but they also see it as a *better* pathway in preparing their child for ultimate success in work and life. Ninety-percent say "you can learn a lot from a job," 89% say "work is important for personal growth," and 85% say "work is important to one's purpose." This strong value placed on work by parents of the coming generation of college students represents a major pendulum swing.
>
> (Busteed, 2019)

I think now, with the benefit of a decade of hindsight, we will look back on the pre–Great Recession modern era in higher education and the post–Great Recession era. The differences are that definitive. By almost any economic measure, life is different for higher education after 2008. Net tuition revenue is down, discount rates are up, and state funding for and support of higher education has dropped significantly. A 2019 National Association of College and University Business Officer (NACUBO) analysis, for example, revealed that average discount rates rose from 31 percent in 2007–08 to over 50 percent in 2018–19 for first-time, full-time freshmen (Valbrun, 2019). According to a report by the Center on Budget and Policy Priorities,

> [a] decade since the Great Recession hit, state spending on public colleges and universities remains well below historic levels, despite recent increases. Overall state funding for public two- and four-year colleges in the 2017 school year (that is, the school year ending in 2017) was nearly $9 billion below its 2008 level, after adjusting for inflation.
>
> (Lenox, 2019)

As costs for higher education continue to outpace inflation, the sticker prices for the most elite private colleges have reached outlandish levels. A recent analysis by the Hechinger Report revealed that several schools, including the University of Chicago, are projected to hit $100,000/year in published tuition by 2025 (D'Amato, 2019). While it is always the case that relatively few students actually pay these sticker prices, the impact on public perception is real. And it is not just the elite schools. A 2019 report on "Trends in Tuition Pricing" by the College Board showed that "[f]rom 1989–90 to 2019–20, average tuition and fees tripled at public four-year and more than doubled at public two-year and private nonprofit four-year institutions, after adjusting for inflation" (College Board, 2020).

All this economic change and disruption has led to a reoriented map and a very different value proposition for higher education at the present moment. Questions of access and affordability are paramount, with presidential candidates and policymakers arguing for versions of free college or loan forgiveness programs. Families and students moving up into postsecondary education are asking hard questions of undergraduate institutions: What are your postgraduate career outcomes? What is the average starting salary of your graduates? How will you help me get a job? The rise of the First Destination Survey (FDS)—which tracks where students land six months after graduation in terms of employment—is a testament to this shift in terms of how outcomes are discussed in higher education. Almost any higher education institution in the United States now publicizes its FDS data on its website, with many touting their successful placement rates. New college ranking systems like those administered by the *Washington Monthly* and Georgetown University aim to rate schools by their return on investment and social mobility rather than simply by institutional prestige as measured by academic standards and selectivity[1]. Again, while these questions have long been on the minds of college students, the Great Recession and its aftermath have brought them to the forefront of the conversation about college choice.

Finally, the economic reorientation and subsequent shift in public perception have had differential impacts on academic disciplines and enrollments. According to 2019 data from the National Center for Education Statistics, the number of degrees in computer and information sciences increased by 50 percent between 2005–06 and 2015–16, while those in health professions and related majors increased by 60 percent between 2010–11 and 2015–16. Conversely,

> The number of degrees in philosophy and religious studies decreased 21 percent between 2010–11 and 2015–16. Also during this period, the number of degrees in English language and literature/letters decreased 19 percent; the number of degrees in education decreased 16 percent; the number of degrees in foreign languages, literatures, and linguistics decreased 15 percent; the number of degrees in social sciences and history decreased 9 percent; and the number of degrees in liberal arts and sciences, general studies, and humanities decreased 7 percent.
>
> (NCES, 2020)

While the pessimism over the practicality of a humanities degree is most certainly overblown (and not supported by at least some of the available evidence[2]), it is the perception that is driving the enrollment reality. The Great Recession and the subsequent economic reorientation have left a public increasingly skeptical about the value of the undergraduate degree and discerning about what kind of academic program and experience make the most sense given the costs. We are told that the contemporary student wants more practical skill development, more real-world connections, and more opportunities to apply what they have learned outside the classroom and the lab. I wonder: When have students *not* wanted these things? Nonetheless, opportunities exist, in this present and economically disrupted age, to imagine new approaches, structures, and pedagogies that meet students (and their families) where they are, even as we continue in our role as educators to help them grow into the individuals, citizens, and scholars they can't yet envision.

THE TECHNOLOGICAL REORIENTATION

The *New York Times* declared 2012 "the Year of the MOOC" (massive open online course). I remember, as a faculty member, reading the *New York Times* piece with incredulity as it described how Stanford University's Sebastian Thrun enrolled over 160,000 students into his online course on artificial intelligence. The number astounded me. In a single moment, my map had been reoriented. How was it even *possible* to teach 160,000 students at the same time?! In a small way, it reminded me of the first time I sent an email to my friend at another institution back in the early 1990s using a (modern at the time) VAX system. I logged on to a computer in the library, typed the message out, added her address, and pressed send. Several moments later, she replied. It seemed like magic. No more stamps! No more expensive long distance calls! But an online course with tens of thousands of students? This was surreal, and it sent shock waves through the sector. Boards told presidents who then told deans to get a committee together to think about MOOCs and their impact on higher education. The craze reached such a fevered pitch that Teresa Sullivan, then president of the University of Virginia, nearly lost her job because of her supposed lack of responsiveness to the technology shifts. College dropout Bill Gates even argued that place-based learning was no longer relevant. At the Techonomy conference in Lake Tahoe, California, in 2010, he quipped, "Five years from now on the Web for free you'll be able to find the best lectures in the world. It will be better than any single university. . . . College, except for the parties, needs to be less place-based" (Young, 2010). Of course, it turned out MOOCs were not quite the revolution everyone thought they would be, but it would be a mistake to dismiss the MOOC craze as merely a fad. Fads and trends are two different things. As Cathy Davidson notes, "That's the trouble with technological change. It's never easy to tell what will or won't last. . . . How do you decide what is the bathwater and what is the baby?" (2017, p. 80).

The MOOC craze was not telling us that higher education would suddenly morph into an online free-for-all, but it *was* signaling profound and lasting shifts in the technology of teaching and learning. It wasn't MOOCs per se, it was the power, portability, and ease of access to learning platforms that represented the biggest change in the higher education landscape. There is a joke that made the rounds on Facebook several years back that went something like this: If someone from the 1950s suddenly appeared in this room, what would be the most difficult thing to explain to them about life today? The answer: "I possess a device, in my pocket, capable of accessing the entirety of information known to humankind." Because this was a Facebook joke post, it concluded with, "and I use it to look at funny videos of cats." It is perhaps difficult to see now, but in the early 2010s, tablets and smartphones were just in their infancy. The first iPhone, for example, was released in 2007 and the first iPad in 2010. Yet now, as Davidson notes,

> [our] students carry smartphones more powerful than the IBM 360 mainframe computers that NASA used to put men on the moon. . . . It's odd and even irresponsible that formal education is the one place where we're not using the devices on which we learn all the rest of the time.
>
> (Davidson, 2017, p. 78)

Before Covid-19, technology in the form of smart devices and online learning was still viewed with skepticism (at best) and downright scorn by many in the academy. This is changing as many of us have been forced into technological spaces and contexts we have long avoided. Nevertheless, we continue to miss the impact of our reoriented maps.

When I graduated from college in 1992, the internet was in its infancy. At one of my former institutions, for example, our "webmaster" was a professor of English who worked on the site in her spare time. Yet just 20 years later, by 2012, one quarter of all undergraduates (4 million students) in the United States were enrolled in at least one class online, and by 2015, 95 percent of colleges and universities enrolling over 5,000 students offered online courses for credit [Shirky (2015) from Davidson, 2017]. As just one example of how far we have come, consider the case of Southern New Hampshire University under the leadership of President Paul LeBlanc who, perhaps ironically, was an English professor before his administrative career.

> Since LeBlanc took over in 2003, SNHU has gone from a little-known third-rate undergraduate business school with 2,800 students, no endowment and a budget that was barely in the black, to America's biggest university by enrollment with 97% of its students online. . . . [SNHU] is projecting a 2020 budget of nearly $1 billion, a surplus of at least $60 million and more than 300,000 students by 2025.
>
> (Adams, 2019)

Prior to 2010, few people could have imagined growth like this.

Now, as faculty in higher education, our daily, lived experience involves things unimaginable even just three decades ago: learning management systems, video conferencing, cloud computing, shared drives, tablets, smartphones, bots, artificial intelligence (AI), Twitter . . . the list can go on and on. Most of these terms of the day would have been unintelligible to a student, faculty member, or administrator at the turn of the 21st century. We, and our students, spend much of our daily lives interacting with screens of various sorts. With the global pandemic, this has taken an extreme turn. I accepted a new administrative position right as the pandemic was hitting colleges and universities in the spring of 2020. I spent my entire spring and summer working at my new institution, while staying at home. I held faculty meetings, attended cabinet and board meetings, and met with students and faculty—all from my kitchen table. After working full time for over four months, I finally met my president face-to-face for the first time since my interview. As I type this, I still have not met most of the faculty face-to-face. I never anticipated I would be a "remote worker" in higher education. Yet, here I am, and here we are. While this new Covid normal may be viewed both negatively and positively in terms of facilitating learning and work, the larger point is that technology was profoundly shifting the teaching and learning experience *before* the global pandemic. In almost all respects, access to information has never been easier. Discrete facts are at our (and our students') fingertips. Our smartphones can now tell us exactly how to get to the museum or the concert in the city and how to avoid traffic. They can even give us our time of arrival down to the minute. Technology has, in many ways, removed uncertainty and risk from aspects of our lives. Our children can call or text us at any moment. If we are lost or in trouble (and crucially within cell phone range), we can instantly find out where we need to go and summon help. We can instantly get directions for soft boiling an egg or watch a video that shows us how to patch a hole in the drywall. As Davidson aptly summarizes,

> The internet and all of the computational technologies developed since its invention harness the interactivity, connection, participation, and access of massive numbers of humans and all the data that we produce, to work at a scale and speed almost unimaginable. It is hard to think of any aspect of our lives that has not been profoundly changed by this technology.
>
> The new education must not only recognize this reality but reimagine higher education that takes advantage of the digital skills our students bring to college while also training them to be full, critical, creative, and even skeptical participants in this technology-driven age. Technophobia is no longer acceptable—in the classroom, in the structures of higher education, in the curriculum, in the pedagogy.
>
> (2017, p. 100)

However, this power and convenience can come at a cost. As Botkin and Davis (1994) argued in *Monster Under the Bed*, there are key differences along the data-information-knowledge-wisdom learning continuum. Easy and ready access to data and information doesn't automatically translate into knowledge and wisdom. In fact, it can result in just the opposite as the recent rise in so-called deep fakes and misinformation social media troll farms have shown. Most of the important things in life do not lend themselves to straightforward answers found in Google searches. How shall I live? Whom shall I love? What makes me happy? Life is open ended and unpredictable. As we learn to work and live, and learn with the technological reorientation of our maps brought about by the internet age, we are left with more questions than answers.

THE DEMOGRAPHIC REORIENTATION

In 2019, I was fortunate to receive a yearlong fellowship with the American Council on Education (ACE). As a fellow that year, I joined a cohort of approximately 40 higher education faculty colleagues from across the country for a year of focused professional development on higher education leadership and administration. It was a crash course in the administrative side of the academy. We would gather together in a typically sterile and chilly hotel conference room and have the chance to hear from national experts on all manner of things, from enrollment management and student life to finance and facility planning. For many of us, one particularly memorable talk came from Dr. James Johnson—a demographer and Director of the Frank Hawkins Kenan Institute of Private Enterprise at the University of North Carolina at Chapel Hill. Dr. Johnson began his talk with us by declaring "demography is destiny" and went on to detail, over the next hour, what he referred to as the "Six Disruptive Dynamics That Will Change America Forever." For many of us in the room, it was an eye-opening session. Personally, I was aware of the general demographic shifts underway in the United States and felt reasonably up to date on the current and potential impacts these changes would have on higher education. But the scope and scale of the demographic changes and their future impacts detailed by Dr. Johnson caught all of us off guard.

The highlights of that talk? First, people are on the move. In the United States, we are experiencing significant population shifts from rural to urban and, generally speaking, from the North and Midwest to the South and West. Combined with these migrations, according to Dr. Johnson, is a rapid "browning" and "graying" of America as a result of immigration, birth rates, and an aging baby boomer population. From 2000 to 2010, for example, the percentage change in terms of population growth in the United States was 1.2 percent for Whites, 11 percent for Blacks, 42 percent for Asians, and 43 percent for Hispanics (Johnson, 2019). In terms of higher education, the non-White student population has grown significantly over the last several decades. According to the National Center for Educational Statistics (NCES), from 2000 to 2017, Black student college attendance rose 5 percent, Hispanic student attendance rose 14 percent, and Asian student attendance rose 9 percent, while White student attendance only increased by 2 percent over that same period. And more change is on the way. In 2014, the non-White student population in K–12 schools in the United States exceeded 50 percent for the first time (Davidson, 2017). The contemporary student moving up into postsecondary education in the United States looks very different from students just a decade or two ago. Today's student, in 2019, is increasingly the first in their family to go to college (first generation), economically less secure, older, female, part time, and non-White. What we once called "nontraditional students" now ought to be referred to as "new traditional" students as they are increasingly the norm on our campuses.

In addition to these changes, there is another key disruption associated with the demographics of higher education that we need to consider—one that has a direct connection to the economic disruptions brought about by the Great Recession. In a landmark analysis and study, Nathan Grawe, a professor of economics at Carleton College, detailed the coming "demographic drop" in the college-age population in the United States. According to Grawe (2019),

Even as we grow to educate a changing student body, another challenge appears on the horizon. In 2008, as the financial crisis raised economic uncertainty to levels not seen in two generations, young families reduced fertility. What began as a sharp pull-back (a drop of about 10 percent in three years) turned into what is now a decade of low and declining fertility.

The result of this decline in fertility is a projected drop in the college-going population by as much as 15–20 percent, depending upon the region of the country. These declines will be felt most acutely in the regions of the United States that are already areas of net migration population loss—the Northeast and Midwest. Yet to Grawe, these demographic shifts are not simply a *fait accompli*. Disruption of these kinds can also be a clarion call for innovation and reorientation:

> What might it look like if higher education were to grow and develop in the face of demographic change such that in 2035 we might say that we did not merely weather a storm but instead stepped more completely into our institutional and societal missions? What if we took actions that not only headed off financial and other disruption but also prepared us for another generation of serving our communities?
>
> (ibid, 2019)

As with the economic and technological disruptions previously discussed, the demographic changes we are experiencing and will continue to experience present both possibilities and limitations. As Dr. Johnson noted, "demography is destiny." Yet, this only tells part of the story. We still have the opportunity to shape the academy those students will experience. The good news is that this reorientation of our maps in higher education presents a tremendous amount of opportunity for new forms of teaching and learning. As Anna Tsing writes in her fantastic book *The Mushroom at the End of the* World, "To live with precarity requires more than railing against those who put us here. . . . We might look around to notice this strange new world, and we might stretch our imaginations to grasp its contours" (Tsing, 2017, p. 3). Given all the disruption and our reoriented map, how might we stretch our imaginations and head off into new and uncertain terrain?

TEACHING AND LEARNING IN UNCERTAIN TIMES

In 2016, a team of four students at Earlham College, a small, liberal arts institution in Richmond, Indiana, where I served as a faculty member for 20 years, participated in a competition called the Hult Prize, which is billed as the world's largest student competition for social good. The prize is sponsored by the Clinton Foundation, and every year the foundation releases a grand challenge for university students to try to solve. What's the motivation? The winning student team receives $1 million to put its idea into action to solve the problem. The grand challenge in 2016 was to double the income of at least 10 million people living in dense, urban areas in the developing world. That's it. That's all the direction students were given. The competition is organized a bit like a spelling bee. Teams of students work on their ideas to solve the problem and then proceed to pitch their ideas to judges at a series of events—first locally, then regionally, and, if they continue to win, at national and international finals rounds. Only the winning team receives the $1 million start-up prize—there are no consolations for second place. Over 24,000 students participated in the 2016 prize competition, and little Earlham College sent its four students and their idea up against the best and the brightest from the top colleges and universities in the United States and around the world. The students named their idea "Magic Bus Ticketing." They developed it after one student, who was from Kenya, noticed the inefficiencies surrounding the public transportation system in Nairobi. The bus system, which involved minibuses and cash, was informal and chaotic—it was difficult for commuting workers to find buses to get to work on time, and it was challenging for the bus drivers to find passengers efficiently. The students devised an idea to use a simple, text-message system that did not require a smartphone (everyone in Kenya used cell phones and SMS in 2016, while smartphone usage with data packages was much less common). Essentially, it was an "Uber for buses" solution using simple texting.

Team Magic Bus, as the student group came to be known, won several local and regional competitions with its idea. That's about when we college administrators started to pay attention. After winning at the national round, the team was suddenly one of only six teams left in the world competing for the $1 million prize in front of President Bill Clinton in New York City. The college live-streamed the final round competition, and students, faculty, and administrators watched as President Clinton walked up to the podium and announced the 2016 winner of the Hult Prize. It was Earlham College.

As an academic administrator working for Earlham at the time, I felt an immense sense of pride in our students' accomplishment. A small, liberal arts school team in "flyover country" had just beat out 24,000 competitors from all over the country and world and had won $1 million to put its idea into practice. It was an amazing moment. However, as a faculty member interested in the scholarship of teaching and learning in higher education, the Team Magic Bus story was illustrative of something else—new and emerging forms and structures for faculty and student engagement and interaction.

The Hult Prize competition at Earlham had been organized through one of our new EPIC centers. EPIC was Earlham's signature initiative for the new liberal arts and stood for the Earlham Program for an Integrated Curriculum.[3] It was an effort to capture the way in which the small, residential, liberal arts experience, when done well, was deeply integrative for students. As those of us who work in higher education know, learning happens everywhere. The distinctive advantage, as we saw it at the time, was in designing an undergraduate learning experience that artfully integrated the curriculum, co-curriculum, and a host of high-impact practice work over four years. The Center for Entrepreneurship and Innovation at Earlham organized the Hult Prize competition at the local level, and both faculty and staff advised the students through the first, early stages of the competition. As things became more serious, the students worked with professors in various disciplines, including computer science, economics, and business, to refine their ideas and their pitch. Significantly, the advising and mentorship extended beyond the teaching faculty to key staff and administrators in career education, advancement, and others as the students worked on their project. The work was intensive and demanding over the course of the year as they went from idea, to draft, to multiple iterations of a final project and pitch. *All* of this work was done outside the classroom and *none of it* was for credit. It involved multiple advisors and mentors, and the students loved it.

As I watched these students achieve this remarkable accomplishment, I was reminded of something Randy Bass, Vice Provost for Education at Georgetown University, once wrote about the changing nature of the teaching and learning environment in higher education. He noted,

> Our understanding of learning has expanded at a rate that has far outpaced our conceptions of teaching. A growing appreciation for the porous boundaries between the classroom and life experience, along with the power of social learning, authentic audiences, and integrative contexts, has created not only promising changes in learning but also disruptive moments in teaching.
>
> (2012, p. 24)

The Team Magic Bus Hult Prize experience involved all the dynamics Bass speaks to in the preceding quote. The project blended the boundaries between the classroom and the real world, it involved social learning through the many collaborations between students, faculty, and staff, and it involved both an authentic audience and a real, demonstrable outcome. However, as Bass suggests, a disruptive question remains in the background of all of this high-impact work: Do most of our formal teaching environments look like this? While there is innovation happening in classrooms and laboratories across higher education (and there always has been), most teaching environments do not fit this mold. In fact, they are its antithesis—individual work with an assigned letter grade in classrooms organized around knowledge transmission, with precious little connection to the world outside the campus. In a disrupted world, a world full of economic, social, demographic, and technological change, does this kind of learning environment prepare students for the challenges they must face? As John Dewey (1916) once reminded us, "education is not preparation for life; it is life itself" (p. 239). Take away the technical urgency for "preparation," and our clarion call is for more "life" in our classrooms and campuses.

Life, these days, is a world full of "wicked problems." In 1973, Horst Rittell and Melvin Webber published an article in *Policy Sciences* titled "Dilemmas in a General Theory of Planning," where they introduced the idea of a wicked problem. To Rittell and Webber, wicked problems are complex, open-ended, intractable problems involving multiple stakeholders and no readily identifiable solutions. Take poverty, for example. We have, in society, always had poverty and it is unlikely (though highly desirable) that we will ever completely eradicate it. It is not, then, immediately fixable through some simple, predetermined solution. In addition, to understand poverty requires bringing in a whole host of interdependent issues and concerns. As Rittell and Webber argue,

> Does poverty mean low-income? Yes, in part. But what are the determinants of low income? Is it the deficiencies of the national and regional economies or is it deficiencies of cognitive and occupational skills within the labor force? If the latter, then the problem statement and the problem "solution" must encompass the educational processes. But, then, where within the educational system does the real problem lie? What, then, might it mean to improve the educational system?
>
> (1973, p. 155)

What Rittell and Webber realized is that once you really start digging into a wicked problem, like poverty, you realize how interconnected it is with other problems and issues. Wicked problems are also problems that have real consequences for real lives, so they are not mere academic exercises. Tackling poverty in a meaningful way will have material benefits for people—it would save lives. The year 2020 has given us two very clear and present wicked problems: a global pandemic and racial injustice. Here, with each of these, we have all the elements identified by Rittell and Webber for a wicked problem: interconnectedness, complexity, open-ended with multiple stakeholders, real consequences, and no simple, single solution at hand. Even as we quickly produce vaccines for Covid-19, for example, we run into more problems. Can we produce enough and distribute them efficiently and fairly? Will people agree to be vaccinated? How will we pay for it? What happens when the virus mutates? These questions are multi- and interdisciplinary and will require expertise from nearly every academic division—natural sciences, social sciences, arts, and humanities.

The same is true in the fight for racial justice. Our students and faculty of color were quick to remind White folks that a rush to "solve the problem" is actually symptomatic of White supremacy. The impulse to make the discomfort go away and quickly get "back to normal" belies the need to stand in witness to the injustices and to both hear and acknowledge the pain, suffering, and wounds caused by generations of racial violence in the United States. How do we solve this wicked problem? What single discipline has the answer? Yet, on the other hand, simply saying, "It's complicated," doesn't permit us to avoid getting to work. Real lives are on the line.

Students coming into our institutions are well aware of many of the wicked problems of the world. While I don't mean to diminish the very real medical truths of our current mental health crises on campuses, I believe at least some of the rise in anxiety, depression, and self-harm among students today can be attributed to their understanding of the world they are inheriting. This is further fueled by social media, which allows us to know, at a more intimate and immediate level, the human (and planetary) suffering that is occurring all around us. It is no longer something you see just once a day on the nightly news or in the daily newspaper the way we might have in generations past. For the contemporary citizen, these problems are integrated and embedded in our media feeds, our story lines, and our notifications. It is an everyday and every moment phenomenon collectively shared (in both senses of the term). It is no wonder students arrive on our campuses and in our classrooms carrying much more than a backpack full of books. And, when the experience in the classroom doesn't speak to their condition, they can often disengage or, in some instances, forcefully demand more. Greta Thunberg, the 16-year-old climate change activist from Stockholm, Sweden, typified this reaction when she walked to the podium at the United Nations in New York in 2019 and said,

> My message is that we'll be watching you. This is all wrong. . . . You have stolen my dreams and my childhood with your empty words. And yet I'm one of the lucky ones. People are suffering. People are dying. Entire ecosystems are collapsing. We are in the beginning of a mass extinction, and all you can talk about is money and fairy tales of eternal economic growth. How dare you!

A world of wicked problems is not patient. It does not wait. And it does not think in discrete, dichotomous ways. It requires the artful integration of knowledge *and* skills; theory *and* practice; depth *and* breadth. But it also demands a certain tolerance for ambiguity—an acceptance of uncertainty and the fact that most of the pressing problems of the world do not come in neat packages with ready-made solution sets. They are messy. They are complex. And they are social. In the end, it isn't about preparing students for the real world. It is about bringing the real world to life on our campuses and, as Bass states, exploring the "porous boundaries" between our classrooms, our lives, and our communities.

CONCLUSION

So, how can we create an environment, in our classrooms and colleges, that more closely resembles and connects with this world of wicked problems? How can we create an educational experience that asks teachers and students to wrestle with ambiguity, complexity, unscripted problems, and multiple stakeholders? As educational anthropologist Dorothy Lee once wrote,

> Are we giving up our heritage of wonder, of curiosity, of questing, of plunging into chaos and creating life out of it? Are we giving up our sense of mystery, the excitement of being lost in ambiguity and building a world out of it?
>
> (1986, p. 42)

Do our present learning environments successfully help students plunge into chaos and create a life out of it? Do we celebrate being lost in ambiguity? We should. Because this is, in fact, more like life. Life is filled with mystery, chaos, and ambiguity, and part of living the good life is learning how to surf these waves. As Davidson aptly puts it,

> As beginning college students or adults returning to school, at various economic levels, and at vastly different institutions . . . students are all asking for the same thing: a new education designed to prepare them to lead a meaningful life in the years after college. . . . The new education must prepare our students to thrive in a world of flux, to be ready no matter what comes next. It must empower them to be leaders of innovation and to be able not only to adapt to a changing world but also to change the world. That is the core requirement of a new education.
>
> (Davidson, 2017, pp. 254–5)

It seems counterintuitive—that to prepare students for an uncertain world, we must create more uncertainty in learning. But this is precisely what we must do. I once heard a scientist talking with young students about the scientific method. She talked about how, in the popular perception of successfully "doing science," the image is always of a white coated researcher throwing papers in the air and shouting "Eureka!" But, in fact, the best and most consequential discoveries more often come from "What the f**k?" moments. Moments when the data make no sense. Moments when we are confused, uncertain, or getting contradictory information. It is in these moments of uncertainty when ideas emerge urging us to go a different way, to take a risk, to reorient the map. How can we help students experience environments that incorporate uncertainty, unpredictability, unscriptedness, ambiguity, and complexity? In order to flourish in this world chock full of disruption, our students need *practice*. Our tendency and habit might be to cling to our old maps, to try to bend them to the new context, to look for stability and lash out against the negative impacts of disruption. But, as Professor Michael Lenox at the University of Virginia recently wrote,

> in my own work on climate change, I have come to view disruption as absolutely critical . . . if we are to mitigate the worst effects of climate change. We need innovators experimenting with new breakthrough battery technology. We need entrepreneurs, like Elon Musk of Tesla, pursuing bold new ventures to upset the status quo. We need established players to disrupt themselves, adopting new business models that lower their environmental footprint. Most important, we need policies and institutions that encourage and support the disruptors.
> So, embrace disruption. Do not fear it. It is necessary and natural. But be critical of disruption as well. Not all disruptions are created equal. Only through the vigorous-yet-critical pursuit of disruption can we create a bold and beautiful future in which we can flourish.
>
> (Lenox, 2019)

In a world of disruption, we cannot lose our most central and important task as educators—to remain vigilant and critical of disruption itself. In our quest to highlight uncertainty and celebrate risk-taking, we cannot succumb to the dogma of innovation for innovation's sake. Uncertainty, as its core, is a rigorous act of intellectual fortitude. To be sure, our maps have been reoriented. But if there is one thing we know for certain, it is that they will be reoriented again. An education that helps students learn that "the map is not the territory" while embracing the discomfort of ambiguity and uncertainty is an education for life. As Wendell Berry (1983), in his poem *The Real Work*, writes, "the mind that is not baffled is not employed. It is the impeded stream that sings."

NOTES

1. See https://washingtonmonthly.com/2018college-guide and https://cew.georgetown.edu/cew-reports/collegeroi/
2. See "AACU . . ." Retrieved from: www.aacu.org/press/press-releases/new-report-documents-liberal-arts-disciplines-prepare-graduates-long-term
3. Earlham College and the EPIC initiative were acknowledged in 2019 by *US News and World Report* as one of the nation's "most innovative" liberal arts colleges.

REFERENCES

Adams, S. (2019). *Meet the English professor creating the billion dollar college of the future*. Retrieved from: www.forbes.com/sites/susanadams/2019/03/28/meet-the-english-professor-creating-the-billion-dollar-college-of-the-future/?sh=228341fb426b

Bass, R. (2012). Disrupting ourselves: The problem of learning in higher education. *Educause Review*, 47(2), 23–33.

Berry, W. (1983). *Standing by words*. Berkeley, CA: Counterpoint Press.

Botkin, J., & Davis, S. (1994). *The monster under the bed*. New York: Touchstone.

Busteed, B. (2019). *This will be the biggest disruption in higher education*. Retrieved from: www.forbes.com/sites/brandonbusteed/2019/04/30/this-will-be-the-biggest-disruption-in-higher-education/#40e1e87c608a

College Board. (2020). *Trends in college pricing: Highlights*. Retrieved from: https://research.collegeboard.org/trends/college-pricing/highlights

Commonfund Institute. (2009). *2008 NACUBO-Commonfund Endowment Study follow-up survey*. Wilton, CT: Commonfund Institute.

D'Amato, P. (2019). *University of Chicago projected to be the first U.S. university to charge $100,000 a year*. Retrieved from: https://hechingerreport.org/university-of-chicago-projected-to-be-the-first-u-s-university-to-charge-100000-a-year/

Davidson, C. N. (2017). *The new education*. New York: Basic Books.

Dewey, J. (1916). Democracy and Education. New York: Free Press.

Friedman, Z. (2019). *Student loan debt statistics*. Retrieved from: www.forbes.com/sites/zackfriedman/2019/02/25/student-loan-debt-statistics-2019/?sh=5d75a388133f

Grawe, N. (2019). *How demographic change is transforming the higher ed landscape*. Retrieved from: www.higheredjobs.com/blog/postDisplay.cfm?blog=25&post=1843

Griswold, A. (2014). *Millennials are the most financially conservative generation since the great depression*. Retrieved from: www.businessinsider.com/millennials-financially-conservative-generation-2014-1

Johnson, J. (2019). Personal communication.

Lee, D. (1986). *Valuing the self: What we can learn from other cultures*. Prospect Heights, IL: Waveland Press.

Lenox, M. (2019). *On words: 'disruption' and 'climate change'? They are connected*. Retrieved from: https://news.virginia.edu/content/words-disruption-and-climate-change-they-are-connected?utm_source=ULinkedIn&utm_medium=social&utm_campaign=news

National Center for Educational Statistics (NCES). (2020). *College enrollment rates*. Retrieved from: https://nces.ed.gov/programs/coe/pdf/coe_cpb.pdf

Rittell, H. W., & Webber, M. M. (1973). Dilemmas in a general theory of planning. *Policy Sciences*, 4(2), 155–169.

Thunberg, G. (2019). *Transcript: Great Thunberg's speech at the un climate action summit*. Retrieved from: www.npr.org/2019/09/23/763452863/transcript-greta-thunbergs-speech-at-the-u-n-climate-action-summit

Tsing, A. L. (2017). *The mushroom at the end of the world*. Princeton, NJ: Princeton University Press.

Valbrun, M. (2019). *NACUBO report shows tuition discounting trend continuing unabated*. Retrieved from: www.insidehighered.com/news/2019/05/10/nacubo-report-shows-tuition-discounting-trend-continuing-unabated

Wheatley, M. J. (2002). *Turning to one another*. San Francisco, CA: Berrett-Koehler Publishers.

Young, J. R. (2010). *Bill Gates predicts technology will make place based colleges less important*. Retrieved from: http://chronicle.com/blogs/ wiredcampus/bill-gates-predicts-technology-will-make-place-based-colleges-less-important- in-5-years/26092

Zezima, K. (2009). *Data shows college endowments loss is worst drop since '70s*. Retrieved from: www.nytimes.com/2009/01/27/education/27college.html

Chapter 3
Students and Uncertainty

INTRODUCTION

One of my responsibilities as an academic administrator at my former institution was to oversee our career area. Every year we would put on a big all-campus event that featured our students giving poster presentations on what they had learned from their summer internships. One year, I was guiding a donor who had helped fund the program around to the various student posters, and we found ourselves in front of "John,"[1] who had just completed a summer internship in Malaysia working for a company involved with something called "supply chain management." At the time, I had never heard of this field—Covid-19 would change that. John was a business major, and, heading into his junior year, he wanted an internship that would give him experience in supply chain management. On the surface, this was a perfect setup. Here we had a student who had chosen his major and was now connecting that major to an experiential opportunity in the form of an internship that would help him develop tangible knowledge, skills, and abilities for his chosen career field. In many ways, this is what the rest of the world expects of higher education and what many students, when they enter college, envision—a simple and straightforward correspondence between a major, their experiences at university, and subsequently finding a job that connects all those dots.

In this particular case, as the donor and I listened, John did a terrific job explaining why he was interested in supply chain management, why he chose this internship, and what he did over the course of the summer working for this company in Malaysia. However, students can sometimes have difficulty moving from the "what" of an experience to the "so what"—why or in what ways the experience was significant. Sensing he had more to say, I asked, "John, what would you say was your biggest personal takeaway from your internship?" John looked at me and then nervously at the donor. He had that look in his eye that said, "Do you *really* want me to answer that honestly?" Often when asking students to reflect, I have found that they tend to give us the answers they *think* we want to hear, rather than the more authentic and messy realities. "It's OK, John," I said, "feel free to be honest." John swallowed hard and took a deep breath. "I realized . . . I don't want to do supply chain management."

Perfect. I smiled and laughed, as did the very successful businessperson-donor beside me. John looked confused. "John," I said, "knowing what you *don't* want to do is just as important as knowing what you *do* want to do!" John relaxed, and we entered into an interesting conversation with him about the messy realities of vocational discernment and the sometimes random and serendipitous nature of developing a career.

In all the talk about making the classroom to career connection more effective and outcome-oriented in higher education today, we can often lose sight of the fact that our highest calling, as faculty, staff, and administrators, is education, not training. With the exception of certain kinds of technical colleges and two-year programs, we are not in the business of *training* students to prepare them for a specific job—our job is to *educate*. Training is prescribed. It is intended to elicit specific skill development, behavior change, and mastery. Education comes from the Latin *educare* and *educere*, which mean to mold, and to lead out, respectively. Education is far more open-ended and process-driven than training. And, as a process, it is inherently unpredictable, uncertain, and emergent.

This can be difficult for students to understand and accept. And before I go much further in a chapter on students, it is important to say that there is no one, universal student just as there is no such equivalent faculty member. I recently read a post on Twitter that argued for referring to "the people in my classroom who are students" to challenge the universalizing way we label. Students are diverse, complex, and highly differentiated in terms of their backgrounds, ideas, values, and preferences—just as other people are. "Student" could refer to an 18-year-old just beginning college straight from high school or a 45-year-old single mother. While both are students, their life experiences share little in common. That said, it would be impossible to say much of use about higher education if we cannot generalize a bit. The point is to do so with some caution and awareness about letting labels get in the way of lived experience.

Present day students are bombarded with messages that tell them there ought to be a tight relationship between their choice of major and a job and that a career is some kind of clear, logical, uninterrupted progression within a specific sector in the workforce. These are rarely true. During admissions events, I often ask parents to raise their hands if they are currently in a job that directly connected to their college major (very few raise their hands). I then ask how many of them have changed careers more than once in their lifetime (many more hands go up). This is not to dismiss the career and job concerns of students and their families. For too long, colleges and universities have ignored the need to more fully integrate career preparation and outcomes into the degrees. As noted in the previous chapter, the Great Recession of 2008 put this oversight into stark relief, and, as a result, we are witnessing a career education renaissance on campuses big and small—from small liberal arts schools to flagship public universities. However, if the message we send to students is that career development is simply a neat and tidy process of organizing a resume and cover letter for that first job (that connects directly to your major) after college, we have done them a grave disservice. Modern career development theory emphasizes the chaotic, serendipitous, and unpredictable nature of vocation and career discernment. The term "planned happenstance" is often used to describe the role serendipity plays in the development of one's career. Mitchell, Levin, and Krumboltz, the scholars who coined the term, argue that,

> [u]nplanned events are not only inevitable, they are desirable . . . being uncertain about goals and wants leads to new discoveries. Counselors need to teach [students] to engage in exploratory activities that increase the probability that they will be exposed to unexpected opportunities.
>
> (1999, p. 118)

If, as Mitchell, Levin, and Krumboltz suggest, uncertainty is not only a given but a *desirable condition* for a successful career, are there ways we can help students engage with the unexpected? What capacities must we cultivate for students to successfully navigate a future that will necessarily be open-ended, unexpected, and filled with uncertainty? As for John, he was convinced that supply chain management would be his career. Yet, during his internship, the unexpected happened. He discovered that he actually didn't like *doing* supply chain management. There are a whole host of uncertainties that crop up for students in college. Some of these are large and potentially overwhelming. How am I going to pay for tuition this semester? Should I report my sexual assault? What if I fail this class? Is climate change going to destroy the planet? Other types of uncertainties are more mundane and every day. What is going on with this data set? What am I going to take next semester? Why does my roommate annoy me so much?

We can break down student experiences with uncertainty into three basic categories.[2] Type 1 uncertainty is uncertainty that is enjoyable and engaging while experienced and in retrospect. As discussed in Chapter 1, the uncertainty that comes from watching a sporting event might be considered Type 1 uncertainty. Type 2 uncertainty is uncertainty that is uncomfortable or unpleasant while experienced, but, upon reflection after the fact, becomes more meaningful, educational, or even enjoyable. Here, we might consider that John's internship amounted to Type 2 uncertainty—it was unpleasant and/or uncomfortable for John to live through the uncertainty of a "failed" internship experience, but, in retrospect, this led to important self-realizations and insights. Type 3 uncertainty is unpleasant or uncomfortable while experienced and, in retrospect, is still unpleasant and noneducative or even miseducative to the person who experienced it. A student who does not know how she will afford next semester's tuition is experiencing uncertainty, but it's not the kind of uncertainty we want to purposefully encourage or design for—students experiencing Type 3 uncertainty are at risk in a whole host of ways. It may be true that some good can eventually come from such difficulties. Living through hard and uncertain times can enhance grit, resilience, and a tolerance for adversity. But chronic or continual uncertainty of this type can be debilitating and is not something we wish to perpetuate or accentuate as educators. So, while there are both positive and negative ways to experience uncertainty, we are interested in designing for and enhancing *productive* Type 1 and Type 2 forms of uncertainty. Simultaneously, we want to work to avoid, or at least not enhance, the kinds of *unproductive*, Type 3 uncertainty students experience.

TODAY'S STUDENTS

Who, exactly, *are* the students of today? Spending time understanding our educational partners is central to creating the kinds of Type 1 and Type 2 uncertainties that inspire growth and learning. In my visits to a variety of college and university campuses, I have always been surprised at the complaint, expressed by some among both faculty and staff, that "we just aren't attracting the kinds of students we used to." Conversation often revolves around a perceived drop in academic preparedness, an increase in mental health challenges, and a greater need for academic support services. Sometimes it will be noted that students today are just not as resilient as they used to be. Buried in these laments is the assumption that, somehow, competitor institution Y has siphoned off a larger percentage of the "good" students, leaving us here at institution X with a greater proportion of the "not-so-good" students. Blame for this state of affairs is often directed at the admissions office and/or the administration and the attempt to attract more students, generate more revenue, and balance budgets. However, a deeper and more challenging explanation of these laments is the implicit biases we harbor about students, about learning, and about excellence. As we learn more about the insidious effects of White supremacy and institutional racism, it is important that we critically examine our assumptions and expectations about students. How and in what ways does "difference" bend too easily in our minds to "deficit"? For those of us who come from privileged backgrounds, have we looked hard enough in the mirror at our own values, thoughts, cultural upbringing, and experiences? Who are we asking to change and why? Bridgette Burns, executive director of the University Innovation Alliance, noted, "We need to stop asking the question: why are the students of today unprepared for college? Instead, we should be asking: why are we so unprepared for today's students?" (2019, personal communication).

That being said, as we discussed in the previous chapter, the demographics of higher education have changed and are changing in profound ways. According to a recent report from the Pew Research Center,

[a]s of the 2015–16 academic year (the most recent data available), about 20 million students were enrolled in undergraduate education, up from 16.7 million in 1995–96. Of those enrolled in 2015–16, 47% were nonwhite and 31% were in poverty, up from 29% and 21%, respectively, 20 years earlier.

(Fry & Cilluffo, 2019)

In addition to the demographic shifts, generational studies and data suggest that today's students, regardless of income and background, come with different values, ideals, and preferences regarding their education. The students we have now are quite a bit different from the students of past decades. And this is not just because more adults and first-generation students are attending college. The students moving into higher education today are bringing new values, attitudes, and preferences with them (as each new generation always does). While generalizations about "the students these days" are always risky, there are data to suggest that millennials and Generation Z have very different attitudes and preferences when it comes to learning and higher education than previous generations. Several years ago, I attended a daylong seminar run by a national marketing firm that specializes in higher education research. They had invited us in order to pitch their services and to help us learn more about the generation of students arriving on our campuses. Defined as the generation born after 1996, Generation Z has a lot in common with the generation before them—millennials, those born between 1981 and 1996. During the meeting, I furiously jotted down notes, fascinated by what I was hearing about the preferences and differences outlined by the marketing firm. The presenters were quick to point out that, with Gen Z, there is no "one size fits all." But they also cited some basic traits of the Gen Z student that I believe are instructive for us as we consider how to meet our students where they are.

- They are hypersensitive to college debt and tend to be savers
- They view technology as an extension of their identity
- They see education as essential to success, and they tend to be college-educated at a higher rate than millennials
- They tend, as a group, to be progressive, open, and equity-minded on social issues
- They value authenticity and are skeptical of being marketed to; they crave authentic, transparent experiences and connections

The top five drivers of college choice for these students are cost of attendance, programs and majors, employability after college, flexible scheduling, and hands-on learning. I came away from the seminar impressed with how quickly things can change and how easy it is to feel "old" after a couple of decades working in higher education. At the anecdotal level, I do feel as though I have witnessed a shift in students in the last decade or so toward the pragmatic—a concern about costs and the usefulness of a degree. On the drive home, I reflected on my own adaptations (or lack thereof) to this new generation of students, and I wondered what more needed to be done. Steve Mintz (2019), professor of history at the University of Texas at Austin, argues,

> The arrival of a new generation of students to campus has forced colleges, time and time again, to adapt. This was the case after World War II with the massive influx of veterans and the sharp increase in women and African American students in the 1960s and 1970s. The more recent inflow of Latino/a, immigrant, international, and low-income students, working adults, and students with disabilities now presents higher education with a new opportunity for renewal and revitalization.
>
> But this will require institutions to be proactive. Colleges and universities must anticipate the challenges they will encounter. Faculty and administrators must reach out to new student populations, listen to their words, and respond in ways that the students find meaningful. Institutions must redesign curricula, delivery modes, support services, and the campus experience itself to meet the needs of a shifting student population.
>
> Colleges, like businesses, must constantly adapt in order to keep up with the pace of change.

That change is constant and that it is here, on our campuses, is a given. Sometimes, however, we have the tendency to think our campus is the exception rather than the rule. But it is not just *our* institution experiencing these changes, it is *all* institutions of higher education. And while complaining about the students you have is a time-honored tradition, it fundamentally fails to adhere to the golden rule of education: You teach the students you have, not the students you wish you had. Blaming students is a form of educational malpractice, and it falls far short of the kind of inclusive and equity-minded mindset we need to help present day students succeed in higher education. During my fellowship year with the American Council on Education, I had the opportunity to spend time with Theo Kalikow, former president of the University of Maine at Farmington and a longtime leader in and advocate for higher education. During a workshop on student success, Theo said something that really struck me by the elegant simplicity of her critique. She remarked, "We fail 50 percent of the students who walk in the door—that is a design problem. What other industry would accept a 50 percent scrap rate!?" (Kalikow, 2019). As Bridgette Burns emphasized, it's not the case that students today are somehow not "college ready." Instead, we ought to consider how our colleges and universities are not "student ready." Our students have changed and are changing—have our approaches to teaching and learning adapted to this reality? Not well enough.

HIGH-IMPACT UNCERTAINTY

Alongside the changes in student demographics and generational preferences, we are learning more about the kinds of experiences students find most meaningful and significant while in school. George Kuh, Professor and Director of the Indiana University Center for Post-Secondary Research, popularized the so-called high-impact practices that are now increasingly a central focus of college and university educational strategies. Drawing on student-reported data from the National Survey of Student Engagement (NSSE), Kuh's work highlights certain student experiences that appear to have a disproportionately positive impact. As Kuh and Kinzie (2018) note,

> The phrase "high-impact practice," or HIP, found its way into the higher education lexicon more than a decade ago. The words signal the unusually positive benefits that accrue to students who participate in such an educational practice, including enhanced engagement in a variety of educationally purposeful tasks; gains in deep, integrative learning; salutary effects for students from historically underserved populations (that is, students get a boost in their performance); and higher persistence and graduation rates.

The differences between students who participated in a high-impact practice and those who did not were so stark and significant that Kuh actually re-ran the analysis several times to make sure the numbers were accurate. Over the last decade, institutions have invested a tremendous amount of time and resources into increasing the quality and frequency of these practices throughout a student's time on campus. The list of high-impact practices from the American Association of Colleges and Universities 2008 report includes the following:

- First-year seminars and experiences
- Common intellectual experiences
- Learning communities
- Writing-intensive courses
- Collaborative assignments and projects
- Undergraduate research
- Diversity and global learning
- Service and community-based learning
- Internships
- Capstone courses and projects

It is interesting to consider what, if anything, these practices have in common. Kuh notes that these activities require purposeful time and effort on task—typically over an extended period of time. They also involve close student-faculty interaction and peer-to-peer collaboration. During these interactions, students often experience frequent feedback and the chance to iterate on their learning. But perhaps most importantly for the purposes of our exploration here, these practices often place students in diverse and novel contexts where they must engage with open-ended questions, with ambiguity, and with uncertainty. To Kuh,

> participation in these activities provides opportunities for students to see how what they are learning works in different settings, on and off campus. . . . While internships and field placements are obvious venues, service learning and study abroad require students to work with their peers beyond the classroom and *test what they are learning in unfamiliar situations*. Similarly, working with a faculty member on research shows students firsthand how experts deal with the *messy, unscripted problems that come up when experiments do not turn out as expected.*
> (2008, emphasis added)

Whether through study abroad, service learning, or undergraduate research experiences, students participating in HIPs often contend with novel situations and contexts where the answers are not readily known or prescribed in advance. There is no neat and tidy pattern of content memorization and one-time test recall of the kind that often occurs in a more traditional class. One doesn't typically "study" for an internship, for example, or take a test on their undergraduate research experience. Most HIPs are immersive experiences that emphasize open-ended trial and application rather than close-ended, after-the-fact testing on fixed content. Throughout the learning process, students participating in well-designed HIPs reflect frequently, make adjustments, and try again. This mirrors much of the style of learning that takes place out in the world beyond the four-walled classroom, and it is perhaps no surprise that students can find it more engaging and impactful. Importantly, follow-up research by Ashley Finley and Tia McNair (2013) found that participation in these practices had disproportionately positive benefits for historically underrepresented students in higher education and that these benefits increased for students experiencing multiple HIPs over the course of four years. What the HIP research shows us is that messy, unscripted learning environments can be some of the most engaging and impactful in a student's career. And significantly, many of these kinds of experiences involve open-ended, uncertain, and even risky contexts for students, and yet the learning can often be profound.

THE BIG SIX

But do the benefits of risky learning like this last beyond the four years of college? The Gallup-Purdue Index provides some intriguing evidence to suggest that they do. The inaugural 2014 study surveyed over 30,000 graduates currently in the workplace about their college experience and correlated that with their workplace engagement and overall sense of well-being. The findings were fascinating. The report states that researchers were unable to find a connection between the kind of school a student attended—public or private, large or small, selective or not—and their workplace engagement and overall well-being. That in and of itself is stunning. The assumption that we carry in higher education in the United States is that the better the school, the better the graduate outcomes. This may be true when it comes to job placement and salary, but the Gallup-Purdue study shows that these factors don't carry over into the more fundamental and important factors like workplace engagement and sense of well-being. There was also no measurable difference between graduates from schools in the top 100 *US News and World Report* rankings and graduates from the rest of the institutions. Given our ongoing obsession with elite institutions of higher learning and the recent "Varsity Blues"[3] admissions scandal, this evidence should give us all pause. Curiously, there *was* a measurable (negative) difference between graduates of for-profit institutions and other graduates, demonstrating that there is at least *some* minimum standard of quality and instruction that matters here. There was also no difference found related to ethnicity, race, gender, or first-generation status.

Yet, despite these variables having seemingly no influence on employee engagement and well-being, six factors *did* show significant impacts. According to the report,

> if graduates had a professor who cared about them as a person, made them excited about learning, and encouraged them to pursue their dreams, their odds of being engaged at work more than doubled, as did their odds of thriving in their well-being. And if graduates had an internship or job where they were able to apply what they were learning in the classroom, were actively involved in extracurricular activities and organizations, and worked on projects that took a semester or more to complete, their odds of being engaged at work doubled also. . . . That these six elements of the college experience are so strongly related to graduates' lives and careers is almost hard to fathom. When it comes to finding the secret to success, it's not "where you go," it's "how you do it" that makes all the difference in higher education.
>
> (Gallup-Purdue Index, 2014)

Given that the study found that only 39 percent of college graduates are engaged at work, these six factors, experienced while in college, have a substantial impact on worklife engagement and overall well-being for our students. We might think of the first three factors as *relational*. Graduates who had a professor who cared about them as a person, who excited them about learning, and who functioned as a mentor were more engaged at work and showed higher overall attributes of well-being. These three elements all revolve around that central and important relationship between an adult (typically, but not always a faculty member) and the student. We might think of the second set of factors as *experiential*. Graduates who had an internship or job that allowed them to apply their learning, who worked on a project that took a semester or more to complete, and who were actively involved in extracurriculars were more likely to be engaged at work. For each of these factors, students were involved in something that connected theory to practice or that enabled them to test themselves out in the arena of life. Like the high-impact practices, these experiential attributes share the common elements of open-endedness and uncertainty. And, perhaps more provocatively, they are rarely located within the traditional domain of the college classroom. Long-term projects, extracurricular activities and leadership, and application of learning in novel contexts are all "off-syllabus" learning activities that do not fit into highly sequenced and scripted lesson plans. Indeed, even the relational attributes in the Big Six have risky elements to them. When students (and faculty) take the risk of building a relationship that goes beyond the shallow and the transactional, the benefits can be long-lasting. A recent metanalysis of 46 studies in K–12 schools found that "strong teacher-student relationships were associated in both the short-term and long-term with improvements on practically every measure schools care about: higher student academic engagement, attendance, grades . . . and lower school dropout rates." And it goes both ways. In another study from the same article, a teacher's sense of joy in the classroom was most strongly correlated to the strength of their relationship with students (Hagenauer, Hascher, & Volet, 2015).

As a parent, I am most concerned about the degree to which my two daughters go on to live meaningful and personally fulfilling lives. Yes, I want them to earn a living, but I mostly want them to lead a good *life*. The Gallup-Purdue data indicate experiences in college that significantly increase the likelihood of leading such a life. The importance of the Big Six experiences is clear but, unfortunately, most undergraduates do not experience them. Of the respondents in the 2014 study, only *3 percent* experienced all six as undergraduates—a shocking and disappointing reality.

Both the Gallup-Purdue Index study and the research on high-impact practices suggest that uncertain learning environments and contexts significantly enhance educational and career outcomes for students. Yet, these kinds of learning experiences are more often the exception than the rule. In fact, where and when they *do* occur, they are often on the margins of what we might call the "formal" curriculum in higher education. This then begs the question: Why? Who, and what, then is the university designed for?

A DESIGN CHALLENGE

It has become somewhat of a standard catchphrase in higher education today to say that, "The university was not designed for students, it was designed for faculty." I have heard many speakers and educational leaders make this somewhat pithy claim, and it always gets a chuckle from the audience. I suspect that many of us, administrators and faculty alike, recognize that many of the structures of academia are outmoded, mere vestiges of the past. Randy Bass, vice provost at Georgetown University, takes this argument even further, questioning the degree to which the formal curriculum ought to remain the center of the undergraduate experience.

> We might say that the formal curriculum is being pressured from two sides. On the one side is a growing body of data about the power of experiential learning in the co-curriculum; and on the other side is the world of informal learning and the participatory culture of the Internet. Both of those pressures are reframing what we think of as the formal curriculum. These pressures are disruptive because to this point we have funded and structured our institutions as if the formal curriculum were the center of learning, whereas we have supported the experiential co-curriculum (and a handful of anomalous courses, such as first-year seminars) largely on the margins, even as they often serve as the poster children for the institutions' sense of mission, values, and brand. All of us in higher education need to ask ourselves: Can we continue to operate on the assumption that the formal curriculum is the center of the undergraduate experience?
>
> (Bass, 2012, p. 24)

Whether it is the academic calendar, grading, registration policies, classroom design, or advising processes and procedures, there is more and more evidence to suggest that we simply have not organized higher education with the student at the center.

As an example, ask a provost or chief academic officer about the distribution of classes across the week, and you will hear the same refrain—too many class offerings on Tuesdays, Wednesdays, and Thursdays between 10 a.m. and 3 p.m. Is this because students *want* classes during these days and times? Unlikely. These are simply the most convenient times for faculty. Another example: Has any research demonstrated that two, 15-week semesters with midterm and final exams are the most effective structure for student learning? I have not seen it. The recent rise in internships as part of the undergraduate curriculum illustrates this tension between the new, decentralized location of learning on college campuses and our traditional systems and structures. As internship participation increases—both voluntary participation by students and, increasingly, as a required part of the major—colleges and universities are struggling with how to account for the activity. Most of the time, internships exist outside the formal curriculum and system of record—causing headaches for department chairs, deans, and university registrars alike. Is it a class? Who is the instructor of record? How do we give it a grade? What term does it fall in? These are all sticky questions that our current system of record often is simply not equipped to handle. The same is true for undergraduate research experiences. All around the formal curriculum, students are increasingly experiencing significant learning—learning that we want to encourage and "capture" in some way, and yet we have a traditional university structure that struggles to account for it.

To be clear, I do not believe faculty, staff, and administrators have somehow conspired to design an organizational structure in higher education that does not support student success. Our historical systems and structures may have made more sense in previous generations. Higher education has served different purposes in different eras. And, we have a culture of incrementalism in higher education rather than disruptive innovation. While we may be committed to liberal education, we are also firmly rooted in conservative organizational structures. As Farrar (2020) notes,

> One thing that has long fascinated me about academe is the tension between its liberal and conservative tendencies. I don't mean politically but in the general sense—our deeply inscribed, dueling impulses toward change and preservation. . . . At the institutional level, for example, we pursue an expressly liberal mission (the open exchange of ideas, academic freedom, accessibility) yet are intensely attached to our bureaucracies and traditions (ponderous governance systems, the hierarchy and exclusivity of our guild).

Yet, despite the many issues surrounding our lack of student-centered design in academe, the blame game is not particularly useful. Most of the faculty I have come across in higher education are hardworking and dedicated to their students and the mission of the university. And, as an academic administrator, I think the "administrative bloat" argument too easily suggests that all of our problems would go away if we just fired most of the administrators and added more lines to the teaching faculty. While there is more than enough criticism to go around, the reality for most institutions rarely fits the stereotypical criticisms for either faculty or administrators. And besides, all this finger-pointing ignores the more central point and issue: How can we work together to better serve our *students*?

MORE TYPE 2 UNCERTAINTY: THE BROCCOLI DILEMMA

Earlier in my teaching career, during a faculty meeting where we were discussing possible changes to general education, a faculty member rose to speak. She was a senior faculty member in the humanities and well respected. Out of the blue, she said, "What we are really talking about here is the broccoli question." She definitely had our attention now. She went on to say,

> there are certain things that our students may not necessarily want to take. They may not know enough yet to know the benefits that come with that

particular way of thinking. It's kind of like what we do with our kids as parents around the dinner table. You may not like the broccoli, we say, but you need to eat it because it's good for you! My department is like broccoli!

That particular statement lived on in the folklore of our institution, and we referred to "the broccoli dilemma" often over the years as we tried to sort through needs and wants for our students within our curricular structure. All sorts of things are like broccoli to our students—certain requirements or distribution-based courses, various styles of learning, and other forms of general "adulting." Students take general education courses they don't like because we faculty have determined that, in the end, those courses will be "good for them." Learning is not always fun. In fact, much of the time it can be challenging, difficult, or uncomfortable. If we are not careful, with all the focus on phrases like "engaged pedagogy," "student-centered," and the like, we can give the impression that teaching and learning are what we might call "edutainment"—a focus on the entertaining and enjoyable side of learning. Certainly, learning ought to be joyous at times and even fun. But it isn't always that way, and one person's fun is another person's worst nightmare. We all have our preferences, but that shouldn't get in the way of what we know to be effective in terms of teaching and learning.

When we consider how students approach uncertainty in learning, there can be times when that uncertainty is not enjoyable or comfortable, even as we recognize (like broccoli) such states of being are, in the end, good for them. I once observed a biology professor working with students in a team-based format. The class was evolutionary biology, and the content for the day was ancient species diversification. Students were separated into tables of four with the faculty member moving among the groups. The instructor began with some basic definitions and an overview of what that day's class was going to entail. This all seemed pretty straightforward to me and not unlike a typical class. But then something strange happened. The instructor gestured to the screen at the front of the room, identified a diversification pattern, and named an organismal group. She then asked the teams of students to draw a cladogram for this particular group that would demonstrate the pattern. The students knew what a cladogram was by this point and had seen a few examples. The students also recognized the organismal order (an ancient order of organisms) from previous coursework. However, the students had never had to put the two things together—knowledge of the family tree and knowledge of large-scale evolutionary patterns. This instructor had been doing team-based learning with this class all semester, so the students knew the drill. They immediately turned toward each and began discussing. The instructor moved between the tables checking in, answering basic questions, and providing background content as necessary. But, importantly, the instructor was not giving them answers. When the students asked if something was "right," she would reframe it as a question: "Well, what might you need to consider if you drew it that way?" There was confusion. There were multiple drafts developed, scribbled out, and changed. In the end, as the tables presented their work, it was clear that there were, in fact, *multiple* ways this particular cladogram could be drawn, depending on both the particular characteristics of the speciation pattern and which traits of the organisms were used in developing the cladogram. This was the meta-point the instructor wanted to bring home. A key concept in biology is that we are still understanding and adjusting key evolutionary relationships based on new information.

What I observed in that particular class were students who were asked to work through uncertainty. They were expected to use past information and understanding and bring it to bear on a new, sufficiently open-ended problem as presented by the teacher. The teacher's job was to move throughout the space, observing students actively working, and ensuring that they understood the previous background content and were successfully integrating it into the new problem. This kind of teaching is, in many ways, riskier. Some students may dislike the fact that they are expected to figure things out without the instructor giving them the answer. They might roll their eyes and say, "Isn't that *the teacher's* job?" Other students may feel frustrated that they have to learn with others. Collaboration takes effort and is harder than taking notes by oneself. Some of this instructor's professional colleagues may wonder what is going on in that classroom when they pass by and see students talking with each other in groups rather than quietly listening to the faculty member lecture. It can look chaotic and disorganized. In fact, in further conversation with this particular colleague, she indicated that she did get pushback from other senior colleagues about the approach. And several students had reacted negatively to the class design over the years. This mirrors some of the research into how students respond to active learning strategies (Tharayil et al., 2018). However, the point of this kind of risky teaching and learning is not to make students uncomfortable or to experiment pedagogically just for the sake of experimentation. These approaches can lead to more effective learning. As this instructor noted to me (personal communication),

> I had a student who complained vociferously in my flipped [class] about how hard it was and how we didn't do any teaching but they had to do all the learning themselves. She then took [another class] in a giant lecture hall the next semester. About a month in, she came into my office to apologize. She had finally gotten the kind of Biology class she thought she wanted (a lecture-based course) and realized that she was not learning the material as well in this teaching format.

Some forms of risky teaching and learning can be derisively labeled as "edutainment" by critics who think that having fun in the classroom means students must not be learning (a curious claim at best). But, as this particular story illustrates, these learning contexts can also be experienced by students as awkward and even confusing, generating student resistance and pushback. When we ask students to practice and produce in this way, it can feel like *work*. It can also trouble dominant stereotypes and perceptions of the teacher-student relationship. The teacher is supposed to be the expert and active, while the students are supposed to be the novices and passive. Paulo Freire (1970) labeled this the "banking method" of education. The teacher "deposits" the content into the empty vessel of the student's brain. Beyond the fact that this is ethically questionable, it is simply not as effective. Shifting from the passive to the active flips the script and the roles. In some forms of risky teaching and learning, it is the student doing the talking and the producing while the teacher listens and monitors. This can be uncomfortable for both the student and the instructor. But, as the story about the student in the biology class reveals, sometimes key, transformative learning comes with some distance from the initial, uncomfortable experience. In our instant gratification, immediate feedback, modern world, we can sometimes mistake our immediate feelings or responses to something as the final indicator of quality. "Quick takes," "Twitterstorms," and "viral" stories all point to the instantaneous judgment orientation of our internet age. This also makes course evaluations completed immediately following a course somewhat problematic. All teachers have experienced that student who five years later writes to us to tell us how they underestimated the value of a particular class that only now is apparent to them. As educators, we know that learning has a way of getting better as it marinates a bit over time. Just like, well, broccoli.

SAFE SPACES AND BRAVE SPACES

As we wrestle with the fact that uncertain teaching and learning environments are not always immediately pleasant or enjoyable, it brings up the question of how "safe" our learning environments are supposed to be. "Risk" and "safety" are antonyms, after all, so how can we simultaneously encourage more risky learning for our students while maintaining their sense of safety? This question of the balance between risk and safety has come to the fore recently as we all wrestle with questions of diversity, equity, and inclusion on our campuses. Frustrated faculty wonder whether they have to significantly curtail or avoid controversial subject matter for fear of having a bias complaint submitted about their class. Students rightly insist that it is not too much to ask that their learning environments be free from racism, homophobia, and other forms of attack on their personhood. Yet, there is a lot of gray area in between these extremes that we are all trying to figure out. Michael Roth, former president of Wesleyan University, recounts a brief history of the notion of "safe space" from its beginnings in the social psychology of Kurt Lewin—a Jewish refugee from Nazi Germany—through 1970s feminism to the more contemporary Black Lives Matter movement and identity politics of the

2010s. Roth's argument is a "both:and" pragmatic move. The caricature made by many in the media and often by the political Right is that the modern university is awash with infantilism and overprotection of students from any kind of context or environment that might make them briefly uncomfortable. Critics revel in stories of "comfort animals," shouted down speakers, and the seeming proliferation of "cancel culture" and language policing on college campuses. However, the reality of the situation is not quite that simple. Roth rightly points out that some forms of safe space practice on campus represent a bridge too far, given the longstanding commitment in academia to freedom of thought and the open exchange of ideas.

> To be sure, there are plenty of examples of sanctimonious "safetyism"—counterproductive coddling of students who feel fragile. Instead of teaching young people to find resources in themselves to deal with chagrin and anxiety, some school officials offer hand-holding, beanbags and puppies. Infantilizing students by overprotecting them, or just treating them as consumers who have to be kept happy at all costs, can be easier and more profitable for institutions than allowing students to learn the hard way that the world is a challenging place and that they have to figure out ways of dealing with it.
>
> (Roth, 2019)

To Roth, it isn't a question of whether or not we should create safe spaces for students on our campuses—it is a question of *what kind* of safety. What he refers to as "safetyism" is a learning environment that strays too far into consumerism and its bedfellows, comfort and satisfaction. There is a qualitative difference between being safe and being comfortable. In its place, Roth suggests "safe enough" spaces.

> As a college president for almost 20 years, I am a strong proponent of creating spaces that are "safe enough" on college campuses. (Here, I draw from the psychologist D.W. Winnicott's concept of the "good enough" parent, who enables a child to flourish by letting them experience frustration and failure within the safety of the family, not by coddling or overprotecting.) Like families, campus cultures are different, but each should promote a basic sense of inclusion and respect that enables students to learn and grow—to be open to ideas and perspectives so that the differences they encounter are educative. That basic sense is feeling "safe enough."
>
> (ibid, 2019)

To return to Roth's central query, we ought to ask ourselves a different question than whether our learning environments are safe or not. We should be asking about the *kind* of safety we are aiming for. Uncertain and risky learning environments often are not comfortable, and they can be quite challenging for students and faculty alike. But it doesn't necessarily follow that they are not "safe." I have frequently said to students when they are upset by something another student said in class, "You don't have a right to not be offended." The awkward double negative aside, I was trying to make the point that difficult dialogue in class may very well result in someone being upset or offended from time to time. That is OK. In fact, introducing productive emotion into the classroom aids memory and retention (Sylwester, 1995). The key is to ensure that the emotions in the classroom are productive and not damaging or counterproductive. When the pulse rate rises and the face flushes due to heightened stress, this is not always a bad thing. The physical responses to stress can vary. In some situations, the brain can productively "upshift" into higher thinking skills and problem solving. In others, the brain response "downshifts" to a perceived threat—what we refer to as a flight or fight response. Some stressful situations, back to Roth, are safe enough. It is the job of the faculty member, in facilitating risky and uncertain learning contexts, to navigate the lines between productive and unproductive stress.

Is safe enough really sufficient as an operational category in light of our present moment? I am not convinced. Safe enough sounds different based upon your lived experience. I believe that our students of color and students from other historically marginalized identity groups deserve more than safe enough. The term itself begs the question, "Safe enough according to whom?" Our campuses have always been safe for cisgendered White males, for example. Why does everyone else only get safe enough spaces? Several years ago on a drive from the airport, I broached this subject with a friend and colleague who was kind enough to pick me up. As a Black teacher and scholar working in a predominantly White institution, she has experienced herself and has seen in her students the negative impacts of various microaggressions. "How do we navigate these differences between what is and should be safe in a learning environment?" I asked. She made a suggestion that I found useful and compelling: "Our BIPOC (Black, Indigenous, and People of Color) students need safe spaces, to be sure," she noted, "*and* it is our job as faculty to *also* create opportunities for them and for all students to be brave—they need brave spaces, too." The combination of safe and brave spaces might help us avoid the kind of safetyism that Roth criticizes, while acknowledging the importance for students, particularly our students of color, to experience a safe learning environment.

CONCLUSION

What do safe and brave spaces look like? As I considered this, my mind wandered back to a time when I felt both safe and brave. One summer, I participated in a mountaineering training course on Mount Baker—a 14,000-foot glaciated volcano located in the Cascades region of Washington state. For a midwestern boy, this was an entirely new environment for me. The landscape was wild—filled with new sights and senses, from the roaring rivers and towering evergreens to the milky whites and blues of the glacial fields. I was nervous. It seemed that all around me there were dangers—falling rocks, snow-covered crevasses, and steep slopes where one slip might mean a serious injury or worse. We spent several days learning the basics down at the toe of the glacier—how to walk with crampons, how to self-arrest using an ice ax, and how to travel safely across glaciers using ropes. On the night of our summit climb, I could hardly sleep. I worried about the dangers I would face and about my ability to actually complete the climb—did I have what it takes to climb all the way up the technical north slope of a 14,000-foot mountain? The roar of the wind through the pines and the unnerving cracking sounds from the nearby glacier seemed to tell me that I did not. We left by headlamp at 2:00 a.m. and slowly worked our way across the glacier and up the north face of Mt. Baker. Somewhere around 12,000 feet, the sun appeared over the horizon, and, for a magical two hours, we climbed on a steep snow and ice slope above the clouds with the warming sun on our backs and a view of the world I will never forget. The position we were in on the mountain was wildly exposed, and I still felt nervous—a fall here would be serious. But I also felt alive, aware, and brave enough to believe that this was a challenge I could successfully complete.

What made me feel safe and brave? There was an experienced guide watching over us. But, crucially, he wasn't doing the work for me—I still had to demonstrate that I could do this climb myself. The rope tied between us offered safety—I knew that if I did slip up, my guide had me and would help arrest my fall. We also dedicated plenty of practice time prior to the final summit push. In the lower risk environment at the foot of the glacier, I learned some of the fundamentals I would need up here at 12,000 feet. However, while my guide was with me and the rest of the group and helped us practice, he couldn't guarantee absolute safety. In fact, several times during the climb, he said in a calm and steady voice, "Watch your technique here" or "Take it slow on this section." I found out later, when I asked him about the climb, that those sections were "no fall zones," as in if we fell there, he would have a hard time arresting our slide because of the precarious position we were in.

Regardless of whether you are climbing a mountain or leading a class, there are certain elements that contribute to the creation of a safe and brave space. This is especially important when we are purposefully designing uncertain learning environments. As with my Mt. Baker experience, roles and responsibilities must be clear in the group. Students need to know the part they play, the part you will play as the instructor, and the impact of everyone's actions on the success of the endeavor. Relationship building early on is critical. After all, on a mountain, your climbing partners hold your life in their hands, and you want to know them beyond just basic courtesies. While a classroom is less directly life-threatening, the impact of relationship and trust building cannot be overstated. I don't know about you, but it is a lot easier for me to be brave among folks I know and can relate to. Additionally, students (and faculty) can move into brave spaces if there are lots of opportunities for "low-stakes" practice. These opportunities build competence, confidence, and trust. The presence of a guide also enables the group to know that someone has been here and done this before, which can provide a sense of a safety net as everyone practices. As faculty, we have to be present with our students as they move into brave spaces, not just physically present but emotionally present. We don't have to always be the expert with all the answers, but we do have to be there. This is the metaphorical rope that connects us to our students. On the mountain, we never went into any risky terrain without "roping up." The rope meant safety; it physically and metaphorically connected us together in a relational and an interdependent way. Rope teams, as they are referred to in mountaineering, must work together to ensure the rope length between climbers stays consistent—not too loose, not too tight. A slip and fall by a teammate necessitates quick reactions and trust that your fellow climber can and will arrest your fall. This requires good communication. Finally, traveling through brave spaces necessitates the guide's constant monitoring of the group with an eye toward success: What does each individual in the group need to be able to succeed? What must we be able to demonstrate before we attempt the high-stakes summit bid?

I did manage to summit that day, as did every member of our team. And our guide reminded us, as we stood on the summit in a congratulatory mood, that we were only halfway. It took us the remainder of the day to make it back to camp exhausted but exuberant. After that first foray into mountaineering, I spent more and more time exploring remote wilderness environments—climbing peaks, snow fields, and ice formations. I was hooked. I remember a time, later in my climbing career, when I was introducing a friend to the sport. We were halfway up a 300-foot sheer rock face on a climb I had done before and that I considered easy. I looked over at my friend and he looked terrified. "How are you doing?" I asked. "I want to go down," was all he could reply. We were experiencing the stress of that climb in very different ways. I kicked myself for not thinking about his beginner status while choosing that particular climb. I had forgotten what it felt like to be a beginner in a risky environment. We decided to bail on that route and try our hand at some easier and less exposed formations.

Our students are graduating into a world almost unimaginable in the scope and scale of its uncertainties. Covid-19, climate change, racial injustice, economic inequalities—there is so much to grapple with. As we recognize the importance of introducing students to a life of productive risk and uncertainty, may we never forget what it feels like to go through it, and may we always stay connected and present with them as they climb.

NOTES

1. The student's name has been changed.
2. Readers might recognize this basic framework from the distinctions made between "Type 1, Type 2, and Type 3 Fun" in outdoor activity. See http://goeast.ems.com/three-types-of-fun/.
3. For more on this, see www.insidehighered.com/admissions/article/2019/09/30/admissions-field-still-coming-terms-varsity-blues-scandal

REFERENCES

Bass, R. (2012). Disrupting ourselves: The problem of learning in higher education. *Educause Review*, 47(2), 23–33.

Burns, B. (2019). Personal communication.

Farrar, M. (2020). *Does pausing your administrative career mean it's over?* Retrieved from: https://community.chronicle.com/news/2290-does-pausing-your-administrative-career-mean-it-s-over

Finley, A., & McNair, T. (2013). *Assessing underserved students' engagement in high-impact practices*. Washington, DC: Association of American Colleges and Universities.

Freire, P. (1970). *Pedagogy of the oppressed*. New York: Penguin Classics.

Fry, R., & Cilluffo, A. (2019). *Rising share of undergraduates are from poor families especially at less selective institutions*. Retrieved from: www.pewresearch.org/social-trends/2019/05/22/a-rising-share-of-undergraduates-are-from-poor-families-especially-at-less-selective-colleges/

Gallup-Purdue Index. (2014). *Great jobs great lives*. Retrieved from: www.gallup.com/services/176768/2014-gallup-purdue-index-report.aspx

Hagenauer, G., Hascher, T., & Volet, S. E. (2015). Teacher emotions in the classroom: Associations with students' engagement, classroom discipline and the interpersonal teacher-student relationship. *European Journal of the Psychology of Education*, 30, 385–403.

Kalikow, T. (2019). Personal communication.

Kuh, G. D. (2008). *High-impact educational practices*. Washington, DC: Association of American Colleges and Universities.

Kuh, G. D., & Kinzie, J. (2018). *What really makes a 'high-impact' practice high impact?* Retrieved from: www.insidehighered.com/views/2018/05/01/kuh-and-kinzie-respond-essay-questioning-high-impact-practices-opinion

Mintz, S. (2019). *Are colleges ready for generation Z?* Retrieved from: www.insidehighered.com/blogs/higher-ed-gamma/are-colleges-ready-generation-z

Mitchell, K. E., Levin, A. S., & Krumboltz, J. D. (1999, Spring). Planned happenstance: Constructing unexpected career opportunities. *Journal of Counseling & Development*, 77(2), 115–124.

Roth, M. S. (2019). *Don't dismiss safe spaces.* Retrieved from: www.nytimes.com/2019/08/29/opinion/safe-spaces-campus.html

Sylwester, R. (1995). *A celebration of neurons.* Alexandria, VA: Association for Supervision & Curriculum.

Tharayil, S., Borrego, M., Prince, M., Nguyen, K. A., Shekhar, P., Finelli, C. J., & Waters, C. (2018). Strategies to mitigate student resistance to active learning. *International Journal of STEM Education,* 5(7). Retrieved from: https://stemeducationjournal.springeropen.com/articles/10.1186/s40594-018-0102-y

Chapter 4
Faculty and Uncertainty

INTRODUCTION

One of the shared responsibilities in the department at my former institution was teaching the senior capstone experience in the interdisciplinary environmental studies major. Following a curriculum revision, the new senior experience involved a yearlong integrated research project where students worked directly with a community organization on a project of demonstrated need. Each fall, we solicited project ideas from the community, with individuals from the local organizations joining us in class to pitch the projects to the students. Loosely based on a model first developed by the University of Oregon,[1] students would then deliberate among themselves about which project sounded the most appealing to pursue. The role of the faculty member, me in this case, was to organize the speakers and project ideas from the community and then facilitate the conversation among the students for the first few weeks of the fall semester to help steer them toward a decision. During the year when I was the instructor of record, we had several project ideas from the city of Richmond—one involving storm and sewer water runoff, one involving urban blight revitalization efforts, and one involving a playground. As the seminar leader, it was not my job to pick the project. In fact, this was meant to be part of the experience for students. As most environmental problems and problem-solving contexts involve collaboration, we wanted students to experience collaboration with each other around something that mattered—in this case, their final, cumulative senior capstone project. But, as faculty, we often have our own opinions about what project might be best for our students. That year, as I sat and listened to the various project ideas and student deliberations, I had one significant thought: "Please don't pick the playground project."

Denise Ritz, the superintendent of parks for the city of Richmond and the person in charge of the playground project idea, was a charismatic and energetic leader. As she pitched the idea in class to the students, I could tell she was winning them over to her project. The playground in question was a small, dilapidated jungle gym made of rusted metal in a public park within walking distance from campus. Denise wanted the students to do a complete renovation of the playground and redesign it especially for children with sensory processing disorders. If this new playground came to fruition, it would be the only playground of its kind within 80 miles. While the students deliberated on the projects, I sat back and silently repeated to myself, "Please don't pick the playground, please don't pick the playground." The reason for this mantra wasn't because I hated children or because I was some scrooge about playgrounds. I just didn't think that the project was intellectually rigorous enough. And I was struggling to envision how we would build a reading list and curriculum around the project. "It's just a playground," I remember thinking, "where is the intellectual weight? We are all going to be bored with this in three weeks."

THEY PICKED THE PLAYGROUND

As faculty in the classroom, we perhaps don't like to use the word "control" when we think about our relationship with students and the curriculum, but, in many ways, this is our proverbial comfort zone. We shape our syllabus, integrate our assignments, and design our unit and lesson plans around specific prescribed aims and objectives. We very much don't want a classroom, lab, or other kind of learning activity that is "out of control." Control, in a pedagogical sense, allows us as teachers to anticipate, to shape, and to direct the learning. We have some sense of how things will go, the sequence of events, and the time frame of the activity. This is why we often talk to newer faculty about the importance of repeating preps. Teaching a course for the first time can be extraordinarily taxing. We can feel punch-drunk, stumbling through unfamiliar material we ourselves are just mastering and a course sequence and flow we have never experienced before. But, after teaching that same course (even with some changes) several times, we become much more comfortable and, well, *in control*. This is not a bad thing.

However, control is a funny term in education. John Dewey (1938) dedicated quite a bit of time to this concept in his writing, and he argued, as he did with so many things, that we are thinking about control in a much too divided way. Control is often viewed in social dynamics as control *over* something—as in my control over the students in the classroom. But to Dewey, control also had to do with self-control. That is, the degree to which the student also could and should experience and enact positive control. In Dewey's framework, control is transactional and relational—it involves both the teacher and the students experiencing control together. If it is taken too far either way, we have a "miseducative" situation (one of Dewey's clumsy but descriptive terms). Too much control from the teacher leaves the students with little sense of agency and engagement. Too much control from the students leaves the learning environment with insufficient direction and purpose.

So, according to Dewey, it is not a question of whether a learning experience is either in control or out of control. Risky teaching and learning is about finding a balance so that students and faculty experience elements of *both*. Without this relational and interdependent sense of control, our comfort and desire for control as teachers can lead to boredom and disengagement on the part of students. They can sleepwalk through the motions of class since everything is already prescribed, anticipated, and accounted for. From the student perspective, everyone sits in the same seat, the professor lectures from the same place, and the material is taken straight from the textbook. While the student is present, there is hardly any room for her to bring herself to the learning given the thick blanket of control thrown over the entire endeavor. It's a play where the script is written, everyone knows their lines, and the ending is predetermined (except, perhaps, the hope that we can get out five minutes early). If you ever want to test how much a classroom environment can become routinized and scripted, sit in a different seat when you enter. Or teach from a different location in the room. The students will look at you as though you have just ripped apart the universe. But control, in the end, only gives us the illusion of comfort and security. Several years ago, a colleague who practices Buddhism gave me a card of encouragement after a particularly rough semester. On the front of the card was a picture of a monk meditating in the midst of a calm and peaceful scene. The caption read, "Relax. Nothing is under control." I put that card on the front of my office door to remind me (and anyone who might walk by and read it) of this deep and fundamental truth.

Somewhere in the fuzzy middle between too much and not enough control is the place of uncertainty. And that was where I found myself in this particular senior seminar. As a participant observer in the process of choosing the capstone research project, I listened and observed the student discussion but I did not direct it. I was in an unusual and somewhat uncomfortable spot of having the responsibility to lead a course and serve as the instructor of record while not knowing what, exactly, we would be doing. The syllabus, as it was, had learning objectives and a rough timeline of general activities and assignments, but there was a whole lot of blank space in between. The course, at this point, didn't feel out of control, but it sure contained a host of unknowns.

I didn't know a thing about designing a playground. As a teacher and scholar, my expertise in teaching this seminar involved my knowledge of social theory— certainly not sensory processing disorders or child psychology. I fretted that I would be unable to offer anything of value to the course and to the students. The class I had in my head involved the group of us diving into the literature of environmental social theory and "problematizing" (such an awful word) the world through the lens of this applied project. As we began the planning, the students decided they didn't want to just *design* the playground, they wanted to see it through to construction and completion. So many questions circled in my head: "Do we have enough time to get the work done?" "Are we going to be able to deliver what the park superintendent and the city actually want and need?" "Did the students pick this project just because it sounded fun and non-academic?" "Will my departmental colleagues view this whole thing as a joke?" I left class that day in a sour mood, thinking dark thoughts about the shallow desires of my students, about my incompetence as a teacher, and about the prospect of a long year working on a potentially silly project. But one of the great things about risk and uncertainty is that, by definition, you never really know how things will turn out.

Once the students decided on the playground, they kicked into gear. Denise, the park superintendent, came back to give us an overview of the scope and scale of the project, and we worked up a Memorandum of Understanding (MOU). We created a project timeline using a Gantt chart. The students were excited to learn and practice these practical and tangible skills. Soon, a weekly pattern emerged. I would turn up to class, and the students would have a list of things they were working on in relation to the project. "Jay," they said one day, "we decided we needed to learn about child developmental psychology in relation to play, so we researched these articles. Can we plan to discuss them next week?" On another class day: "Jay, we don't know anything about fundraising, can you invite someone from the Development Office to class to give us a primer?" One Tuesday I turned up and they said, "Jay, we need to learn computer-aided design. Can you see if the library has a software license for Sketch-up Pro and someone who can train us on it?" Throughout the year, I was essentially the class errand boy—tracking down experts and resources or helping find readings that provided the background knowledge and content for the project. Occasionally, I served as the project manager, reminding them of how to plan with the end in mind, stay on task, and manage the inevitable intergroup conflict that arises on projects like this. Several times throughout that year, I privately doubted whether the students could pull it off or whether I was playing the right role as the supervising faculty member. "What if they miss their deadlines?" I would ask myself as I watched them squabble over whose turn it was to take notes. "What happens if they don't fundraise enough for the city to move forward on bids?" "How am I going to grade this?" There was a real chance this project, and the whole senior capstone year, could collapse under the weight of it all. I felt like a stage director who wonders whether the cast and the play will be ready by opening night. The pressure was on, and all I could do was offer encouragement and the occasional suggestion about how to work effectively as a team. My silent, repeated mantra shifted from "please don't pick the playground" to "please don't screw this up."

As the months went along and winter lost its grip on campus, things began to come together in that small seminar room on the second floor of Dennis Hall. Remarkably, the students took to fundraising like a child to a free swing set. It turns out that having students ask for money from the usual big pocket donors in the community is far more effective than when a government official does. The park superintendent was thrilled. And I began to notice something. The students were actually *learning*: not just about sensory processing disorders but about the environmental psychology of outdoor play, about public parks and issues of access and inclusion, and about the connections between quality of life and sustainability. In addition, they were also acquiring *skills*: how to fundraise, write proposals, complete an MOU, use computer-aided design software, and work through a city government Request for Bid (RFB) process. And it turned out that I could, in fact, create assignments and assessments related to the work that I could grade. "You know," I thought one day as I watched them work, "all this is going to look great on their resumes." We had come a long way from my initial skepticism about the potential learning that could come from a project about a children's playground.

By the end of that semester, somehow, some way the students had pulled it all together. On a rainy Friday afternoon, the day before graduation, the students, with Denise's help, had organized a big reveal ceremony for the playground at the local National Guard Armory across the street from the park. There, surrounded by community leaders and supporters, the students unveiled their design and the latest fundraising totals. All told, they had raised over $200,000 for the sensory playground, now called "A Playground With a Purpose."[2] They had selected a vendor through the city RFB process based on their design, and the entire playground was slated to be installed and completed over the summer. They had done it, and I felt like a proud parent sitting in the back of the room as the students received accolades and applause from city officials and local leaders.

And, in October of that same year, many of them made a special trip back to Richmond so that they could be present at the official opening of the playground. With community members present, the now graduated students looked on with pride at the new community resource they helped bring to reality. One of them even gave a tear-jerker of a speech. Several weeks later, the president of our college contacted me. He told me that he had just received a note from a mother who said that she was writing with tears in her eyes because now, for the first time, she was able to take her son to a playground in Richmond that was safely designed for him and his learning differences. She thanked the college for being such a great help and support to the community. Needless to say, the president was thrilled, and I was reminded, once again, of the power of uncertainty in teaching and learning.

THE UNCERTAIN TEACHER

A story like the Playground With a Purpose might suggest that teaching and learning with uncertainty is a simple choice: Just stop trying to control everything, let your hair down, and go for it! But, as we have discussed, uncertainty and its bedfellow, risk, are more complicated than that. There are reasons why, as faculty, we elect to take the safe and more certain pedagogical paths. As with students, some types of uncertainty for faculty are better and more useful than others. We might think about a faculty member's day-to-day experiences with risk and uncertainty as generally falling into three categories:

1. Intellectual uncertainty (disciplines, new knowledge, learning curves)
2. Social uncertainty (colleagues, students, policies, practices)
3. Self-uncertainty (fear, self-doubt, failure)

And, while not always true, uncertainty can grow deeper and more complex as we move down the list. We tend to be more comfortable as faculty, for example, with intellectual uncertainty than with social or self-uncertainty. Regardless of the discipline we teach, every field, area of study, and way of knowing accepts and appreciates a certain amount of epistemological uncertainty and intellectual discomfort. In fact, we encourage this with our students in various ways. Several years ago, I had a revealing chat with a colleague of mine who is a molecular biologist. She talked about how, given the field, students in introductory classes had to learn how things worked based upon a certain foundation of knowledge. However, as they advanced in their studies, faculty had to admit to them that what they had learned in their introductory classes was out of date given the current research and they would have to "unlearn" it in order to understand where the field had moved in its understanding of biological structure and systems. This fascinated me. At some point, faculty had to basically state: "Much of what we have taught you to this point is wrong." This same faculty member later sent me a report from the Academy for the Advancement of Science that put this intellectual uncertainty into disciplinary perspective:

> As biology faculty, we need to put the "depth versus breadth" debate behind us. It is true today, and will be even more so in the future, that faculty cannot pack everything known in the life sciences into one or two survey courses. The advances and breakthroughs in the understanding of living systems cannot be covered in a classroom or a textbook. They cannot even be covered in the curriculum of life sciences majors. . . . The time has come for all biology faculty, but particularly those of us who teach undergraduates, to change the way we think about teaching.
> (American Association for the Advancement of Science, 2009, p. XV)

Our fields are constantly changing and, as academics, we inherently understand this dynamic. New information in the form of research, theory, technique, or style moves from margin to center and changes the way we understand and, eventually, teach our fields. At times, such changes can be uncomfortable, but, by and large, this is a domain we are familiar with as scholars. In fact, many of us chose our profession precisely because of the enjoyment and fulfillment we receive working in a place that values lifelong learning. This is not to say that intellectual uncertainty is comfortable. Debates about disciplinary versus interdisciplinary knowledge, for example, can get quite heated. Arguments and challenges to dominant paradigms in various fields often involve significant risk-taking and can lead to a great deal of emotional turmoil and angst for scholars in the field. But, much of the time, uncertainty of this kind is just part of the job and is actually quite often engaging for faculty.

When moving from intellectual uncertainty to social uncertainty, things get a bit trickier. Social uncertainty, as I am categorizing it here, involves the risk and uncertainty for faculty associated with their interactions with the people, policies, and procedures within a given institution. It is important to note, as with students, not all risk-taking and uncertainty is to be sought after and celebrated in the life of a faculty member. The risk and uncertainty involved with promotion and tenure, handling challenging relationships with colleagues and students, and various forms of microaggressions and implicit bias for faculty members of color—all these and many more situations of social uncertainty in the day-to-day life of faculty can be unpleasant, if not downright hurtful, oppressive, and professionally damaging. A colleague of mine at another school, who identifies as a person of color, sat down over coffee with me and spoke about this issue. She noted,

> some professors who are white guys like you can have students call them by their first names and it's cool. But for Black people, you know, there are Black scholars and researchers who still walk into their buildings, offices, and classrooms and people call security. They think we don't belong here. My point is that uncertainties look different depending on where you are situated in terms of race and other categories of identity.

Contract faculty, adjuncts, and other part-time or contingent teachers may look at risk-taking and uncertainty in ways that are quite different from tenured and tenure track faculty. Folks who work in the community college environment or primarily with first-generation students experience risk-taking in their teaching in different ways than faculty might in predominantly White institutions or with students who come from privilege. In short, we cannot simply celebrate risk-taking and uncertainty in the social sphere without acknowledging and understanding the larger societal dynamics that frame them. While we cannot control how individuals (students, faculty, staff, trustees, etc.) behave and respond to uncertainty, we should think carefully about policies, procedures, and systems that support healthy risk-taking and uncertainty and actively combat unhealthy forms of the same.

Earlier in my career, I served as a Teagle Teaching Fellow for the Great Lakes College Association. My role, as a fellow, was to help advance the science and art of teaching and learning on member campuses through the dissemination of research and best practices, as well as to visit campuses to host discussions with faculty. During one of these campus visits, our group of fellows sat down with a group of pre-tenure faculty members at the institution. As we discussed their challenges with teaching, a common and shared frustration emerged—they were very unclear about the institutional expectations around tenure. Many of them reported receiving mixed messages about the balance of research, teaching, and service. It was clear to us, as we listened, that the climate of social uncertainty at that particular institution was making it hard for faculty to embrace risk-taking in the classroom. Here, the institutional policies, procedures, and culture around tenure created a form of social uncertainty that was not conducive to healthy risk-taking. In Chapter 8, I will discuss how colleges and universities can change policies to encourage healthier risk-taking and uncertainty in teaching and learning, but, for now, it is worth stating that, for a variety of reasons, faculty experiences with the social uncertainty in higher education tend to be more complex and perilous than our experiences with intellectual uncertainty. And these experiences can pose a real challenge to faculty as they consider how to encourage more risky learning for students.

THE FEARFUL TEACHER

Beyond intellectual and social uncertainty lies a deeper and more fundamental form of uncertainty that can get in the way of faculty taking more risks in teaching. Rick Reis, who blogs on faculty development under the title Tomorrow's Professor at Stanford University, notes,

How receptive faculty are to changing their pedagogical approach is a complex issue, but one factor that impedes change is the fear of taking a risk. Underlying this fear may be the fear of loss, fear of embarrassment, or fear of failure.

(Reis, no date)

Self-uncertainty acknowledges that at least some of our reticence to take risks comes from our own "stuff"—our previous experiences, our self-belief, and our mental outlook. And, as we discussed in Chapter 1, perception of risk (and potential loss) is highly individualistic. We see this with our students—some may be perfectly comfortable raising their hand and asking a question in class, while others may be terrified at the prospect. One student may look forward to working in a group, while another will beg and plead to work independently to avoid it. What is deemed risky by one can be easy for another and vice versa. In a general sense, self-uncertainty has to do with the fear of loss. The loss experienced can be technical in nature (such as loss of classroom control or loss of time on task) or it can be more personal—a loss of "face" or in other words shame.

Losing time to cover content to take more pedagogical risks and allow more uncertainty to enter into the classroom is a common fear. Time, as we know, is the currency of the realm for faculty, and dropping content in favor of new methods and approaches is a risk many are not willing to take. In my many conversations with faculty encouraging them to try out active learning strategies, for example, I have heard variations of the following: "I have too much to cover to spend time doing that." "My field is too content-rich and highly sequenced for that to work." "Our discipline and our accrediting body require that we cover specific content so we have no room for trying something like that." However, the reality is that, except in rare circumstances, we really don't have to cover everything we think we do. And we might ask how much of what we cover students actually retain. Why do we constantly speak of "covering" content, anyway? Shouldn't we instead try to set up contexts where our students "uncover" the content? There are examples in virtually every field I am aware of—from physics to classics, from nursing to biochemistry—where faculty have successfully incorporated uncertainty into the classroom and lab.

I often ask faculty, when they talk about the importance of content coverage, "How much do you think your students will remember a year after they took your class?" This often elicits a strange look. I follow that with another question: "If you saw a student walking across campus and they approached you excitedly saying, 'Dr. Ramirez! I just wanted to thank you for that class I took with you last year. I'll never forget about. . . .' What is it that you hope that student would say next?" That second question often gets faculty going. They will respond with wonderful and compelling goals and purposes for their course. I recently had just such a coaching conversation with an assistant professor of linguistics. During our time, she spent the first half discussing, at length, the many topics and content areas she felt she had to cover with her students. I listened patiently until she finished. She then stated, "But the thing is, I am noticing that only a small percentage of my students are actually engaged in class." I followed with the two-part question described earlier in this paragraph, and when I described the serendipitous meeting with a student a year later, she thought for a second and replied, "I hope she would talk about the realization that, every time we open our mouths, it provides a window to our world." "All right!" I said. "Design your course with that as your primary objective. How can you elicit that understanding at a deep level?" For the rest of the time, we talked a whole lot less about all the content she wanted to get through in this course and a lot more about the concepts and understanding she wanted her students to be able to demonstrate and what experiences would elicit them. This shift to demonstrating learning is the mindset and process behind McTighe and Wiggins's (1998) Understanding by Design (UbD) model.

Yet underlying the fear of loss of control or time is a deeper and more fundamental form of fear: the fear of shame and embarrassment. To understand why we have a fear of taking risks, we have to understand the psychology of fear itself. Karl Albrecht (2012) describes the five main types of fear we all share:

1. Extinction
2. Mutilation
3. Loss of autonomy
4. Separation
5. Ego death

Most of these (hopefully) we don't have to worry about in our day-to-day lives as faculty, although Covid-19 has added a fear we thought we would never have to endure in our profession—that the act of teaching in the classroom might actually be life-threatening. But Albrecht's description of separation and ego death get right to the heart of where fear shows up in teaching. By separation, Albrecht refers to "the fear of abandonment, rejection, and loss of connectedness; of *becoming a non-person*—not wanted, respected, or valued by anyone else." Ego death, on the other hand, is "the fear of humiliation, shame, or any other mechanism of profound self-disapproval that threatens the *loss of integrity of the self*; the fear of the shattering or disintegration of one's constructed sense of lovability, capability, and worthiness" (Albrecht, 2012, emphasis in text).

Parker Palmer, in *A Courage to Teach*, explores this particular issue in depth. To Palmer, the fear of taking a risk is simply the outward expression of our deepest fears—the fear of being "found out" as a sham, inadequate, incapable, or incompetent.

> In unguarded moments with close friends, we who teach will acknowledge a variety of fears: having our work go unappreciated, being inadequately rewarded, discovering one fine morning that we chose the wrong profession, spending our lives on trivia, ending up feeling like frauds. But many of us have another fear that we rarely name: our fear of the judgment of the young.
> (Palmer, 2007, pp. 47–8)

As college faculty, we spend our lives in modes of public speaking in front of some of the most judgmental folks alive—our students. This is not to blame students. In fact, we help *train* them to be judgmental and critical. And we often misperceive students as being more judgmental and harsh than they actually are or intend to be. The classroom interaction that we obsess over was likely forgotten about by the student as they walked out the door. Palmer argues that we tend to cope with this fear by erecting a range of protective armor around ourselves: credentials, an air of expertise and aloofness, or good old-fashioned cynicism. Even the traditional physical classroom setup with a podium and rows of seats provides a degree of protection against the fear of judgment.

Early in my career, I remember waiting with bated breath for the course evaluations to be returned to my office after grades had been posted. This was usually right before a break (either winter or summer), and it was one of the last things I would do before I left the office for the semester. My wife would always know how those evaluations turned out because they inevitably influenced my mood and attitude for the first week of break. I would open the interoffice manila envelope with anticipation, my heart skipping a few beats, as I scanned the comments and marks. The kind and positive comments would wash over me as an affirmation that yes, in fact, I was a *good* teacher. But inevitably, those weren't the comments that I focused on. What I was really focused on were the zingers—and there were always some. As I read, they would flash before me like those animated captions from the old Batman TV show: "I found myself more interested in watching the squirrels outside the window than in Jay's lectures." Bam! "Jay seemed to play favorites in this class." Whack! "I got nothing from this class—total waste of time." Pow! The ratio of positive to negative comments could be 10:1, but I would still come away focused on that one zinger comment and wind up feeling like an incompetent teacher. I had a hard time, as a young faculty member, separating my teaching self from my self-self. A negative comment about my teaching was a negative comment about *me*. Questions would inevitably follow: Was I good enough? Did I belong at this school? Did I belong in this profession?

Perhaps even worse than the fear of judgment that comes from students is the fear of that same judgment coming from *colleagues*. Listen to many faculty and, while they may say they are nervous at times speaking in front of students, they will talk about how much *more* nervous they are speaking in front of their peers. And, of course, we have designed a system in higher education that amplifies that fear through the tenure and promotion process. In order for us to retain our job and receive tenure, we must prove our worth as a scholar and teacher to our colleagues. For those not on the tenure track, we still must actively demonstrate our competence and worth through annual reviews at contract time. The system seems to be designed to incentivize playing it safe. Young faculty are told to "keep their head down." Contingent faculty are told to "not make waves." Some faculty who try new techniques or methods in the classroom can find themselves in trouble with senior colleagues who don't appreciate the "showboating." Other faculty may be told to "focus on your research" and not spend so much time on teaching. Student course evaluations and teacher performance review processes are rarely designed to acknowledge and celebrate risk-taking. Try something new as a pre-tenure or contingent faculty member and you risk tanking your student opinion of instruction scores—something that could significantly impact your contract renewal. So, it is important to recognize that this fear of judgment is not *unfounded* for faculty. There are real consequences to risk-taking for faculty—both tenure-track and contingent. And, we must note again that risk-taking for faculty members from historically underrepresented groups—people of color, LGBTQ, international, and women—can be especially challenging.

So, teaching is hard enough as it is: Why would we make it *harder*, or more uncertain, by taking risks? Because playing it safe can also be, paradoxically, risky—both for us as faculty and (importantly) for our students. There can be a *cost* to playing it safe. It is as if there is a mutually agreed upon set of rules in the classroom. The students won't make too much of a fuss so long as the professor doesn't try anything unusual. The script has already been written, the rules are clear, and everyone simply has to act their part. The problem is that the "act" is often just that—an act that can lead to a learning experience that is passive, inauthentic, and disengaging. And all of this feels safe. But often, this classroom dynamic occurs not because we want to feel safe but because we give in to fear. To Palmer, "having been wounded by fearful young people who hold their teachers at arm's length, these teachers fearfully fend off their students, thus feeding the cycle of fear" (2007, p. 48). When we give in to this, all of us, students and faculty, lose. We lose our creativity, our energy, and our passion. So how can we break the cycle of fear?

THE RISKY PASS

As a fan of soccer (football to everyone outside the United States), I watch quite a few games (especially when Liverpool plays—my favorite team from the English Premier League). One of the things you notice when watching a game is how players show up on the field. Often, a player may start strong but make a few wayward passes or mistakes. Suddenly they begin to disappear from the game. They don't "show" for the ball as much (invite a player to pass to them). When they have the ball, they play the safe pass (usually sideways or backwards). It becomes a bit of a self-fulfilling prophecy. The more they play it safe, the more they shrink from the field. The more they shrink from the field, the more other players stop passing to them. Commentators notice this and mention how a player has "gone missing" in a game. Inevitably, coaches see this too and make a substitution. What the coach needs is for that player to understand how and when to take risks. Failure is a part of it. Players who show for the ball, who are willing to take on opponents with an offensive dribble, and who will try a risky pass often experience failure— their moves and ideas don't always come off. But without these failed moves and attempts, the overall objective doesn't get met—creating a chance that leads to a goal. Playing safe usually means losing the game.

The opportunity costs of playing it safe in our teaching are well known. We go missing from the game when we stop learning. Faculty speak about colleagues who have "let their field pass them by." Students complain about that professor who has used the same set of lecture notes (or, these days, slide deck) year after year. Teachers find themselves saying things like, "I just don't understand the students these days." As we prepare for a new semester, we too easily fall into routinized course designs and assignments. Perhaps we occasionally think of new ideas or maybe a bigger revision, but then we inevitably choose the sideways pass—we shrink from the field. We play it safe. We get comfortable being comfortable.

After teaching for ten years at the institution where I had spent the bulk of my professorial life, I began to feel the temptations of comfort. I had made it through the tenure process, and, as an associate professor, I was established at the college, reasonably well liked and respected by students and faculty, and in my groove. It was all going great. But I was also beginning to feel a creeping sense of boredom with the routine. I read papers from students that reminded me of the exact same paper and argument from a previous semester. Class days would come and go in a predictable rhythm. I wasn't happy with the level of engagement and performance from students in some of my classes. Things needed a refresh. I was fortunate enough to find a professional development opportunity through our academic consortium funded by the Teagle Foundation to embark on course redesign. The Teagle project asked us, as faculty, to take an existing course and redesign it connected to emerging research on the neuroscience of learning. As I considered one of my courses in particular, I kept going back to experiences I had had with students while leading off-campus study programs. Students almost always seemed truly engaged and transformed in these programs, experiencing learning that was quite impactful and often life changing. I wondered why. The research from the neuroscience of learning suggested that social and emotional dimensions play a critical role in both knowledge acquisition and retention (Bransford, 2000). This made intuitive sense to me as I thought back on my off-campus semester experiences with students. The students seemed to get so much more from the experiences because they were laden with emotional moments and social components—the cohort experience of traveling and living with their classmates, the trials and uncertainty of their homestays and internships, and the out-of-class experiences that helped connect course content to the so-called real world. All of these elements seemed profoundly powerful to those students and created a strong, emotional connection to the place (in this case, the community of Whanganui in New Zealand). As I considered the Teagle project, I kept thinking, "Why can't we create these same feelings and outcomes back here in Richmond, Indiana?" Most of our students came to Earlham from elsewhere, and there was a longstanding negative attitude about the local community. I wanted to see if we could change that. However, all the things that worked in an off-campus program were not easily replicable on campus. "We can't do those things during an on-campus semester course," I would say to myself. "This would be crazy . . . and too much. Just tweak it a bit." I wanted to play it safe. But a little voice in my head kept asking, "Why not try?"

I PLAYED THE RISKY PASS

I decided to redesign my course around the principles I thought worked in the off-campus study space: cohort building, experiential assignments and opportunities, and what Richard Kraft (1992) called "strange-land experiences" in the community. My Big, Meaningful, Audacious Goal (BMAG) was to move students from a deficit mindset about Richmond to an asset mindset. Richmond would become a place the students viewed as a positive resource for them in their college career. Importantly, it was not just about designing fun experiences.

I wanted to create an effective emotional and social learning environment that enabled students to learn and retain the key course content better through the course redesign. With the support of the other faculty in the Teagle project, I went to work trying to mirror as much of the off-campus experience as possible in the course. We used the local river (the Whitewater) as our focus and metaphor (the course was on the concept of place in environmental thought). We spent a weekend camped out on a local, multigenerational family farm. We did a service project cleaning up a section of the river. On another day, we traveled from the "tip" to the "tail" of the river, beginning at the headwaters and finishing at the confluence with the Ohio River near Cincinnati. We brought in local experts to talk about various aspects of the river—historical, ecological, and social. We visited the wastewater treatment plant. I had to get over my fear of loss as all this transpired: fear of losing control over the class and the student experience (what if all these field trips bomb?); fear of losing too much content (how can we *not* read anything from Casey!?); and, at a deeper level, fear of failure (what if the students think all this local engagement is a waste of time and it reinforces their negative attitude about Richmond?). And fear of ego death: What if they think *I* am a waste of time? What if they express that to their friends and other faculty? The gremlins of doubt were really going now.

There were some failures along the way. Some of the local experts were less than engaging. A few students had to skip out on some field trips for various reasons and, as a result, missed out on some of the key emotional and cohort-building aspects of the course. The tip to tail day had to take place on a Saturday, and it was a LONG day for all. But at the end of the semester, when I opened up the interoffice manila envelope and read the course evaluations, I was stunned. The students not only talked about what they liked and didn't like, but they also reflected on the impact of the course on their lives—how it made them look at Richmond differently and how they were now thinking about their relationship with their own hometowns differently. They also spoke about how this course made them seriously consider changing their major to environmental studies and how they wanted to be more involved in place-making activities in Richmond and wherever they would call home later in their lives. Some described the course as the most important one they had taken in college thus far. There were also things they thought went less well—the course asked too much of their time in spots, the field trip days had to be changed several times for various reasons and that led to confusion about the schedule, and some thought the assignments were not clear enough. It was not a perfect course. But in reading through the evaluations, it was clear that my risk—to try to replicate an off-campus experience on-campus—was worth it. And, just to reemphasize that pedagogical risk-taking is never completely triumphant, there were still a few zingers thrown in for good measure.

THE VULNERABLE TEACHER

So how do we dance with fear? If we acknowledge that risk and uncertainty are a necessary part of teaching in higher education (not to mention just being human), are there strategies and approaches that can help us and, by association, our students be more comfortable with being uncomfortable? Whether the uncertainty we face is intellectual, social, or self-directed, there is a concept that can help that may, at first, seem counterintuitive. Buddhist nun Pema Chödrön writes,

> anyone who stands on the edge of the unknown, fully in the present, without a reference point, experiences groundlessness. That's when our understanding goes deeper, when we find that the present moment is a pretty vulnerable place and that this can be completely unnerving and completely tender at the same time. What we are really talking about is getting to know fear, becoming familiar with fear, looking it right in the eye—not as a way to solve problems, but as a complete undoing of old ways of seeing, hearing, smelling, tasting, and thinking.
> (Chödrön, 2008, p. 52)

Chödrön is asking us to become more comfortable with the feeling of vulnerability. This, as I said, can seem counterintuitive. When I am dealing with uncertainty and the attendant fear, the *last* thing I want to do in that moment is be vulnerable. However, it turns out that vulnerability is an excellent way to work with fear and uncertainty. Brené Brown, in her book *Dare to Lead* (2018), writes about what she calls the "arming behaviors," like blaming, shaming, cynicism, perfectionism, and emotional stoicism, that get in the way of our dance with fear and uncertainty. She writes, "Our daily lives are defined by experiences of uncertainty, risk, and emotional exposure. There is no opting out, but there are two options: You can do vulnerability, or it can do you" (Brown, 2018, p. 24). By vulnerability doing you, she means the ways our arming behaviors serve as an attempt to protect against the feeling of vulnerability. Instead of being vulnerable and taking accountability, we blame others. Instead of being vulnerable and accepting that sometimes we fail, we strive toward perfectionism. Instead of being vulnerable and allowing emotion to be part of our teaching, we portray a stoic persona in the classroom.

Brown's books are targeted toward the C-suite executive set, but her breakdown of what she calls armored leadership as opposed to daring leadership provides a useful and compelling frame within which to think about how we might dance with uncertainty and embrace risky teaching and learning with our students. She writes,

> As children, we found ways to protect ourselves from vulnerability, from being hurt, diminished, or disappointed. We put on armor; we used our thoughts,

emotions, and behaviors as weapons; and we learned how to make ourselves scarce, even to disappear. Now as adults we realize that to live with courage, purpose, connection—to be the person we long to be—we must again be vulnerable. We must take off the armor, put down the weapons, show up, and let ourselves be seen.

(Brown, 2018, p. 78)

To Brown, armored leadership (teaching in our case) involves a range of compensating behaviors driven by fear and seeking to avoid vulnerability. She juxtaposes these behaviors with what she calls daring leadership, which provides the orientation needed to show up and be seen.

Armored Leadership	Daring Leadership
Perfectionism and fear of failure	Empathy and self-compassion
Being a knower and being right	Being a learner and getting it right
Hiding behind cynicism	Modeling clarity, kindness, and hope
Hustling for our worth	Knowing our value
Leading for compliance and control	Cultivating commitment and shared purpose
Weaponizing fear and uncertainty	Acknowledging/naming fear and uncertainty

Is this easy to do? Absolutely not. What Brown calls daring leadership, we might call risky teaching. The attributes in the right-hand column are, in some senses, simple to understand, but they are not easy to enact. Simple and easy are not the same thing. One example of this is a blog I found several years ago from Sonya Huber (2014) titled "My Shadow Syllabus." In it, she lists 42 points that she wants her students to know about her as the classroom journey begins. It is a deeply vulnerable and emotional piece—something we normally do not bring into a conversation about how to properly build and introduce a syllabus to students. However, in her shadow syllabus, Huber models what we have been exploring here about taking risks and asking our students to do the same. Several of my favorites from this piece include the following:

> The goals and outcomes I am required to put on my syllabus make me depressed; they are the illusion of controlling what cannot be controlled. . . .
> Our flaws make us human; steer toward yours. I steer toward mine. That won't always be rewarded in "the real world."
> One of you who is filled with hate for this class right now will end up loving it by the end.
> One of you who I believe to be unteachable and filled with hate for me will end up being my favorite.
> One of you will drive me to distraction and there's nothing I can do about it.

Later I will examine the reason you drive me to distraction and be ashamed, and I will then try to figure out my own limitations.

Secret: I get nervous before each class because I want to do well.

Secret: when I over-plan my lessons, less learning happens.

Secret: I have to plan first and THEN abandon the plan while still remembering its outline.

Secret: It's hard to figure out whether to be a cop or a third-grade teacher. I have to be both. I want to be Willie Wonka. That's the ticket. Unpredictable, not always nice, high standards, and sometimes candy.

(Huber, 2014)

Of the three types of uncertainty discussed in this chapter—intellectual, social, and self—it is self-uncertainty that is the deepest and most difficult to address. But, the counsel from Palmer, Chödrön, Brown, Huber, and many others who think and write on the themes of risk, uncertainty, and self suggests that facing our fears, with all the courage and the vulnerability we can muster, is worth it—for us and, crucially, for our students.

NOTES

1. For more on the model, see the Sustainable Cities Institute: https://sci.uoregon.edu/
2. See https://earlham.edu/playground-with-a-purpose/ for more on this project.

REFERENCES

Albrecht, K. (2012). *The (only) 5 fears we all share*. Retrieved from: www.psychologytoday.com/us/blog/brainsnacks/201203/the-only-5-fears-we-all-share

American Association for the Advancement of Science. (2009). *Vision and change in undergraduate biology education: A call to action*. Retrieved from: http://umdberg.pbworks.com/f/Vision-and-Change.pdf

Bransford, J. (2000). *How people learn: Brain, mind, experience, and school*. Washington, DC: National Academies Press.

Brown, B. (2018). *Dare to lead*. New York: Random House.

Chödrön, P. (2008). *Comfortable with uncertainty*. Berkeley, CA: Shambhala Publications.

Dewey, J. (1938). *Experience and education*. New York: Collier Macmillan.

Freire, P. (1970). *Pedagogy of the oppressed*. New York: Continuum.

Huber, S. (2014). *My shadow syllabus*. Retrieved from: https://sonyahuber.com/2014/08/20/shadow-syllabus/

Huston, T. (2009). *Teaching what you don't know*. Boston, MA: Harvard University Press.

Kraft, R. J. (1992). Closed classrooms, high mountains and strange lands: An inquiry into culture and caring. In K. Warren, M. Sakofs, & J. Hunt (Eds.), *The theory and practice of experiential education* (pp. 8–15). Boulder, CO: Association for Experiential Education.

Kuh, G. D. (2008). *Excerpt from high-impact educational practices: What they are, who has access to them, and why they matter*. Washington, DC: Association of American Colleges and Universities.

Palmer, P. J. (2007). *The courage to teach: Exploring the inner landscape of a teacher's life*. San Francisco, CA: Jossey-Bass.

Reis, R. (n.d.). Preparing faculty for pedagogical change: Helping faculty deal with fear. *Tomorrow's Professor Blog*. Retrieved from: https://tomprof.stanford.edu/posting/696

Wiggins, G. P., & McTighe, J. (2005). *Understanding by design*. Alexandria, VA: Association for Supervision and Curriculum Development.

Part Two

Teaching Through Uncertainty

Chapter 5
The Uncertain Classroom

INTRODUCTION

How do you make learning about concrete interesting? This was the challenge Dr. Armen Amirkhanian, assistant professor of engineering, chose to tackle at the University of Alabama. As a licensed professional civil engineer, Dr. Amirkhanian already believed that concrete was interesting, of course, but his challenge was to transmit that interest and passion to his students. The class in question was CE262 "Civil Engineering Materials." Armen was a Learning in Action Fellow[1] participating in a faculty development program focused on the university's Quality Enhancement Project (QEP) in experiential learning and problem solving. I got to know Armen while I was serving as a consultant for the project over the course of several years. As a fellow, Armen would meet with me to talk through his ideas on course redesign in light of the project goals to increase experiential learning opportunities for students and to improve problem solving. The course in question, was serving as his redesign project, and Armen was interested in making the course more experiential and applicable in the real world. "I was trying to take the engineering lab on concrete, which was already hands-on and experiential, from prescriptive learning to actually experiencing the learning process," he recounted. As he participated in the fellowship program, Armen had a sense that, while the lab portions of his course were hands-on and active, they were missing something. "In the past, students literally had a step-by-step recipe to follow, like you are baking a cake, to make a really good concrete mixture."

As we talked about his course, his learning goals, and this particular lab, I asked him, "What if, instead of giving them a recipe, you just told them to try to figure it out using the materials at hand? What if you put an uncertain experience *first* and brought the content in afterwards?" Armen became intrigued about what I have termed the "experience before label" approach. It was clear that the past designs of the course and the lab were just not engaging enough, and, importantly, the learning environment was not something they would actually see and experience

DOI: 10.4324/9781003029809-7

77

in the field as future engineers. He went about redesigning his lab with this in mind. Describing his new approach, he noted,

> Usually the students would enter the lab and they would just read off the sheet and follow the instructions. But, I didn't do that this time. What I did instead, before we even got to the concrete portion in lecture, was to get them into the lab and tell them: "make me concrete." I didn't tell them the proportions, I didn't tell them what ratios. I just said, "Go mix it."

Armen recalled, "When they mixed it, all sorts of crazy stuff happened. Some had sand. Some had soup. But they all learned something."

Armen was so impressed with this simple change from the recipe-based approach to the "make me concrete" approach that it became part of a larger course redesign. He noted,

> Three weeks after that lab, they learned how to go through the mix design process in lecture and how to do the proper calculations. We then expanded that work into a final project where students were given a set of specifications from the Alabama Department of Transportation (ALDOT). They actually had to design a component that met realistic strengths—they literally had ALDOT specifications in front of them and they had to understand how to use testing techniques to meet those specifications.

Armen wanted to make sure students were experiencing some of the uncertainty and ambiguity that occurs in day-to-day engineering work.

> The students had to read through a very technical document and sometimes these can be a pain to read. Specification documents are often 20 pages long but you might only need one paragraph in order to do your work. Figuring out what is optional and what is mandatory takes interpretation.

He did note several challenges. A few of the students were annoyed that they weren't given a sheet of paper that told them exactly what to do. "I told them to get over it and think about why I am not giving them a recipe to follow," Armen recalled.

> It was very unstructured, overall. I did tell them they could Google how to make concrete in the lab if they wanted to but those that did wound up with a bad mixture. That's because your concrete mix depends on the kind of aggregate you use and that can vary quite a bit. It showed them you can't just Google the answer.

It was clear, listening to Armen, that he had succeeded, not just in making concrete interesting but in designing a learning environment and set of experiences for students that were engaging, challenging, and relevant. When I spoke to Armen again after his initial pilot redesign, he seemed on fire about his new approaches. His students were more engaged, and he was excited about the potential and possibilities not just for this course but for other courses he taught in the department as well. Armen had even begun presenting on this work at regional and national conferences. And it all began with a small shift in how he taught a simple concrete materials lab.

I love Armen's story because it illustrates how a simple change to put immersive, uncertain experience first and content second can yield big dividends. This chapter is about how we, as teaching faculty, can try out changes both big and small to introduce more uncertainty into learning. In doing so, we take risks and we ask our students to take risks with us. Importantly, bringing elements of risk and uncertainty into the classroom is not simply "winging it." It takes careful design and preparation. But isn't it somewhat paradoxical to plan for the unexpected? Perhaps. In my experience, there are, in fact, methods to the madness and we will explore them next.

NAVIGATING THE METHODS MORASS

Every teacher has been through the experience of hearing about an innovative pedagogical method that is lifted up in a faculty retreat as the great new approach to solve all our various teaching woes. Those of us involved in teacher education and faculty development don't necessarily help with our emphasis on a growing set of jargon and models to describe pedagogical innovation. A scan of the contemporary discourse in the scholarship of teaching and learning in higher education reveals a "word salad" of such jargon:

Problem-based learning	Active learning
Project-based learning	Team-based learning
Game-based learning	Applied learning
Design thinking	Experiential learning
Community-engaged learning	Inclusive pedagogy
Universal design for learning	Competency-based learning

When these methods get trotted out in a faculty retreat or workshop, teachers can listen to them with a skeptical or perhaps even cynical ear. First, these methods often get set against "traditional" ways of teaching. And, too often, traditional can be perceived as a proxy for "bad." If we are not careful, simplistic dichotomies can be created. In one variation, traditional teaching is equated with lecturing (which must be bad), whereas nontraditional teaching is equated with innovation (which must be good). Or we can juxtapose active versus passive learning in simplistic ways that ignore the variation and methodological diversity in between. And while there is a developing body of research that supports the educational effectiveness of many of the methods listed previously, there are also studies that raise important concerns and critiques (Prince, 2004). Faculty rightfully can and should question the taken-for-granted language used in the scholarship and discourse of teaching and learning, as well as the assumptions underlying the proposed methods.

On the other hand, another false dichotomy can develop—one where new approaches are described as unproven or vacuous "edutainment," while traditional methods are seen as time-tested and rigorous. Our language can get in the way here. The term "lecture," for example, is a curious one. We use it as both a noun ("I am going to hear a lecture") and a verb ("She lectured for two hours"). Outside of academia, lecture is often viewed negatively. No one wants to *receive* a lecture, for example. Lately, the lecture has come under quite a bit of scrutiny. The *Chronicle of Higher Education* trots out article after article predicting its demise or defending its effectiveness.[2] But what is a lecture, exactly? Is it simply standing behind a lectern and speaking? Is it a specific form of instruction? Does it just mean outdated and ineffective teaching? I have observed plenty of lectures that were engaging and educationally effective for the students in attendance. Rarely did these experiences involve only the professor speaking. There was always interaction between students and the instructor in the form of questions and answers, paired shares, clickers, or in-class reflective assignments. Lecture, to me, is an unhelpful descriptor of what we do in classrooms. I prefer to borrow a term from the K–12 context and use the phrase "direct instruction." It is more descriptive of a particular type of teaching that can occur episodically in (and out) of the classroom. Direct instruction occurs when the instructor is speaking (with or without visual aids) directly to students and introducing or reinforcing content. It mostly (but not exclusively) involves the teacher talking and the students actively listening and perhaps even (shock!) taking notes.

It is not the case that one *either* lectures *or* does active learning, for example. These methods are not mutually exclusive. There are plenty of teaching and learning environments that involve *both* periods of direct instruction *and* periods that are more interactive and/or student-driven. The somewhat tongue-in-cheek rule about direct instruction is that one should limit periods of direct instruction based on the age of the student. A 5-year-old, by this logic, can sit still and focus for about 5 uninterrupted minutes of direct instruction (if you are funny and have candy). For those of us in higher education working with 18- to 21-year-old students, that means we should limit direct instruction to 20-minute periods broken up with other forms of interaction (this also goes better if you are funny and have candy).

SMALL TEACHING

Regardless of the various descriptors, methods, and terminology used in the contemporary literature of teaching and learning innovation, to ask someone to change how they teach can be a challenge. Who among us would respond with enthusiasm if someone were to say to us, "I think you should reinvent yourself!" But, often, this is what can be heard by faculty when we roll out a new pedagogical method or approach. Tony Robbins infomercials about personal transformation to the contrary, we don't often radically and easily change who we are in our day-to-day lives. Why would we expect to do so in our teaching? In his wonderful book *Small Teaching*, James Lang (2016) discusses how relatively modest changes in our teaching approaches can yield big results. Lang writes about how, as a baseball fan, he was struck by the concept of "small ball." Small ball is a concept and strategy in baseball whereby a team tries a number of relatively minor measures—like advancing the runner from one base to the next through bunts, sacrificing flies, or stealing—rather than attempting bigger impact moves like asking a hitter to try for a (more difficult) home run. As a strategy, "small ball" is actually quite effective in baseball. Lang began to think about whether the same concept might apply to teaching:

> My reflections on this . . . led me to consider whether I should incorporate into my workshops more activities that instructors could turn around and use in their classrooms the next morning or the next week without an extensive overhaul of their teaching—the pedagogical equivalents, in other words, of small ball.
>
> (Lang, 2016, p. 4)

As I thought about the promises and pitfalls of the various "new" methods listed earlier, I kept going back to Armen's concrete mixing lab. When Armen thought about how he wanted to redesign his course, it wasn't a radical reinvention that made the difference, it began with a small but powerful change in one aspect of one lab within his course. He changed the sequencing of his lab to enable open-ended, unstructured exploration *first*—before any form of direct instruction. And, he got rid of the recipe-style cookbook approach to making concrete. These were not radical reinventions. They were really just small tweaks to the sequence that were fairly easy to design and implement.

Was Armen's approach active learning, experiential learning, or problem-based learning? Does it really matter what we call it? It demonstrated, to me, not the power of this particular method or that, but the power of messy learning—of unscriptedness, open-endedness, discovery, and even confusion in educational design. And as I thought about the role of uncertainty in teaching and learning,

I began to see how it serves as something of a warp thread through so many effective methods and approaches. Whether we are talking about high-impact practices such as internships, off-campus study, or service learning or emerging pedagogies such as project-based learning, experiential learning, or active learning, uncertainty and the learning characteristics that come with it often play a central role. Perhaps we need to focus less on the jargon and more on the common characteristics that these approaches share that make them particularly effective. One of those common characteristics, in my view, is uncertainty. And we need not reinvent ourselves as teachers to try to incorporate more uncertainty in learning. Relatively minor changes, Lang's "small teaching," could yield significantly improved outcomes and results in terms of student engagement and performance. The more I thought about it, the more I was convinced that there was something to this idea of designing *for* uncertainty in learning in small ways that might lead to bigger "aha's" down the line. We so often try to avoid uncertainty or take it out of the classroom, lab, or learning situation. But what if we have that all wrong? What if, rather than trying to remove it, we actively design for it?

THE PLAYLIST FOR UNCERTAINTY

If we think there may be something to this idea of designing *for* uncertainty, how do we go about doing it? What are the common design characteristics and components of a pedagogy for uncertainty? There is some temptation, at this point, to reply as my father did on Facebook after I posted a general callout for interesting readings and sources on the topic of uncertainty. He replied, "I am not sure about this." Is it not somewhat of an oxymoron to describe, with certainty, what a pedagogy for uncertainty would entail? This would be true if the argument was that there was some sort of formula or lockstep technique to implement. But, like Armen's recipe for concrete, how we mix together all the various components depends very much on context—what you might be teaching, who you might be teaching, and how the various ingredients come together. If we wanted to create more productive and educative uncertainty in learning, how might we go about designing for that? What are the common ingredients?

As I explored the scholarship of teaching and learning literature and interviewed colleagues across a range of disciplines and settings, common themes that contribute to a well-designed, uncertain learning environment emerged. And, as I considered Lang's recommendation to focus on small changes a faculty member could make that would yield big results, I began to formulate some design principles and gather together "small ball" ideas—approaches I have used myself, techniques I have learned from other colleagues, and concepts worth considering from the literature on teaching and learning. All of the ideas are ones I have used successfully in the classroom myself, and many have been incorporated successfully by others as well. That said, as I began to work on this chapter, a nagging feeling kept creeping in: Who am I to tell others how to teach? Should I really focus on techniques and approaches that I have used? Who is to say they will be useful to others? It was then that my daughter came to my rescue. My 14-year-old daughter is very into music, and one day, while we were doing the dishes together, she turned on a playlist she had made so that we could listen to something while working in the kitchen. Usually, I am not a huge fan of her musical preferences, but, in this case, I enjoyed many of the selections. I asked her about it, and she said, "I made this playlist from songs I thought you might like." Right then, a lightbulb went off in my head. A *playlist*. What is great about a playlist is that, while it is personal to the individual that made it, it can also be shared. And, in sharing it, the receiver still gets to decide what songs they like and what songs they perhaps don't care for as much. A playlist is never presented as the only kind of music in the world or the best—it is simply a compilation of songs that one person finds meaningful in some way or another. And, when a playlist is constructed and shared, it is often organized for the person receiving it—what they think that person might like or enjoy.

This helped me get over my reluctance to share these ideas as though they were the final answer to all of our teaching conundrums. I am not sharing definitive and universally proven strategies here. Rather, I am presenting a playlist that I have compiled over the years—a "Playlist for Uncertainty." Having presented this playlist in a range of venues in higher education—from the National Humanities Center to large universities and small liberal arts colleges, I can say that most faculty seem to find something useful in it—a song they like or an approach they would be willing to try. I have organized the Playlist into three categories: Designing for Uncertainty, Facilitating for Uncertainty, and Common Traps. These approaches are unabashedly practical in orientation, and all have been tested and used in the classroom many times. That said, there will be some that you find more useful or interesting than others. That is fine. Copy what you want and build it into your own playlist.

I. DESIGNING FOR UNCERTAINTY

The strategies I have categorized under "Designing for Uncertainty" all have to do with how we go about designing our courses, units, or classes with the conscious and purposeful inclusion of elements of risk and uncertainty. Doing this well places a premium on design because the content often takes a back seat to the experiences the student is having with the content. Without careful design, an uncertain learning environment can seem (and actually become) chaotic, disorganized, or disconnected from learning outcomes. With good design, those same elements of chaos and messiness can be purposefully incorporated into the learning outcomes for the class or unit. Productive uncertainty, it turns out, requires a plan.

BACKWARDS DESIGN

Backwards design is a tool often used in Understanding by Design—a design approach introduced by Grant Wiggins and Jay McTighe in their book of the same name. Wiggins and McTighe describe the approach this way:

> An approach to designing a curriculum or unit that begins with the end in mind and designs toward that end. Although such an approach seems logical it is viewed as backward because many teachers begin their unit design with the means—textbooks, favored lessons, and time-honored activities—rather than deriving those from the end—the targeted results, such as content standards or understandings.
>
> (2005, p. 338)

For Wiggins and McTighe, beginning with the end in mind means thinking *first* about the enduring understandings and key learning outcomes a teacher wants for a given unit or course. Only after articulating those does a teacher then carefully plan and integrate the course content and activities that will elicit those understandings. When designing for uncertainty in learning, this approach is key as it forces us, as faculty, to stay aligned with our outcomes. The temptation at times with a focus on experiences for students is that we end up designing a host of interesting activities that may, in fact, solicit uncertainty and healthy risk-taking but are not, in the end, connected to learning outcomes. By designing with the end in mind, we keep outcomes front and center. Uncertainty, after all, is a means to a larger end—not the end in and of itself. Ask yourself: "What do I hope my students remember one year after taking this course?" I sometimes talk about this as the Big, Meaningful, Audacious Goal or BMAG. Every course should have a BMAG—something you want to happen in the course that is big enough to really matter to you as a teacher. Sometimes we lose sight of what it looks like to really stretch and go for something in a course or in the classroom. The doubt creeps in, and we settle for something more "reasonable." When I work with faculty, I will often say something like, "If your BMAG doesn't make you slightly nervous or anxious, it is probably not big enough."

INTEGRATED COURSE DESIGN

Related to backwards design is another useful framework to consider as you design for more uncertainty. Dee Fink's (2005) Integrated Course Design framework places three spheres of design in relationship with one another: learning goals, teaching and learning activities, and feedback and assessment (see Figure 5.1).

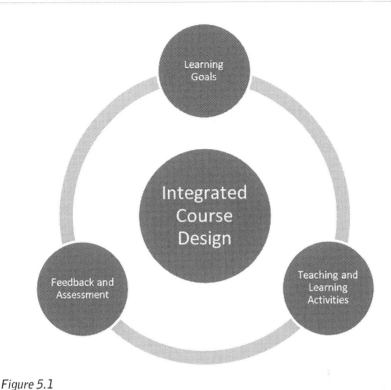

Figure 5.1

Fink summarizes the framework this way:

> The basic components in this model of Integrated Course Design are the same as those found in other models of instructional design . . . formulate the learning goals, design the feedback and assessment procedures, and select the teaching/learning activities. What is distinctive about this model is that these components have been put together in a way that reveals and emphasizes their inter-relatedness.
>
> (2005, p. 2)

Fink's integrated approach reinforces the idea of backwards design, while placing that approach into a larger context that includes teaching and learning activity and assessment. How this can be useful to a teacher who wants to incorporate more productive risk and uncertainty into a course is the way you can integrate those activities and experiences with the broader design aims of the course—both the learning goals and the assessment. As with backwards design, Fink's framework can act as an important check on the temptation to design a project, develop an active learning component, or incorporate service learning without integrating that activity into your goals *and* how you plan to give feedback and assess the degree to which students are demonstrating those learning goals. Ask yourself: "How do the activities and experiences I wish to incorporate into my course integrate with my learning outcomes, and how will I know if students are getting it?"

EXPERIENCE BEFORE LABEL

Of the many strategies I have introduced to faculty over the years, "experience before label" is one that is most often cited by workshop participants as useful. I think it is because it is a simple concept (Lang's small ball again) but with a big potential impact. As teachers, we have been trained to reverse this strategy—give the label first and then perhaps offer a chance for students to experience something related to the label. This is true in the sciences when we lecture first and then have students in the lab. It is often true in the social sciences and humanities when we go through a unit or engage with a text, and then afterward have students write a paper or perhaps go on a field trip of some sort. We are socialized into this structure and order and for good reason—it makes sense in a logical and sequential way. But learning and understanding are not often like that. By putting the experience first, we are asking students to make sense of the inherent messiness of learning. We want them to explore first. This is a central tenet of inquiry-based learning: Begin with open-ended exploration and questioning, and then move to content and concept labels. Armen's concrete lab serves as an example of how to do this in small ways all the way down to the lesson plan level. This is important as we aim to design more risk and uncertainty into our teaching, because unscripted and messy experiences, what Dewey called "the indeterminate situation," often serve as the creative engine for learning. You can also think about putting the experience before the label on a larger scale. How might we put the experience before the label as we design an internship? A study away course? As we design the course requirements for a major? Or within our general education program?

COLLABORATIVE COURSE DESIGN

A classic teacher joke goes something like this: "I designed the perfect curriculum but they sent me the wrong students." There is a nugget of truth in this joke that has to do with the curiosity that, even in our current so-called student-centered paradigm, we continue to design and plan our courses *in advance* of meeting our students. This makes sense, of course, given how schedules are made and how the entire operation of school works—whether K–12 or higher education. But it is worth noting that this is actually not a great way to create an effective learning environment. Perhaps the ultimate, risky teaching we could do as faculty is to show up on day one and *not* have a completed syllabus to deliver to students. This is the idea behind collaborative course design. What if the students worked with us to design the course? How might that even work? In my own classes, I have taken various approaches to this design idea. For introductory courses, where students may not have enough background knowledge to weigh in with specific ideas, I often dedicate a class or two to question generation. Splitting students into teams, I ask them to generate as many questions as they can about the subject matter for the course. I encourage them to simply brainstorm—no question is out-of-bounds or inappropriate. I also tell them that these questions will help guide how we move through the semester, so that they see this not as a trivial exercise but as a way to build a shared and collective sense of ownership over how the course will be organized and run.

In upper-level courses where students may come in with more understanding and experience, I often ask them to suggest units we could focus on. Or, I give them a draft syllabus and we workshop the design together—what is missing? What could be emphasized more? What topics are you most interested in? As our students continue to push us to think more about ideas surrounding inclusive pedagogy, diversity, equity, inclusion, and anti-racist education, the collaborative design approach opens up possibilities for increased student agency and ownership of the learning. And you might be surprised at what the students know and how they can help make the course design better, more inclusive, and more diverse both in content and in structure. Does it come with risks? Of course. But, in my experience, the rewards of even a small amount of collaborative design work outweigh the risks. We sometimes expect too little of our students. Give them the opportunity to weigh in and collaborate with you on the course and I think you may be surprised.

II. FACILITATING UNCERTAINTY AND LEARNING

The next set of concepts and strategies relates to how we can best facilitate and process learning through risk and uncertainty. The word "facilitate" comes from the root *facile*, which means to "make easy." Learning through risk and uncertainty is inherently uncomfortable. It is incumbent upon us, as instructors, to facilitate learning in such a way that students can move through that discomfort successfully. This requires a set of skills and strategies that we are not necessarily taught in graduate school or in your average teaching and learning workshops. We may have *designed* a lesson, a unit, or a course with uncertainty in mind, but if we don't actively facilitate that lesson, course, or unit, we can fail to achieve the desired outcomes for our students.

THEIRS TO OURS TO THEIRS

I first learned of this facilitation concept from work I did with an organization called Learning Forum, which ran summer academic enrichment camps for students who needed extra support. As teachers in the program, we had to understand that the mental models many of these students were bringing into the classroom were things like, "This is going to be boring." "I am probably going to fail." "Nobody knows or cares about me." We were trained, through this program, to mitigate these negative frames by purposefully starting in their world—the world of the students—*before* inviting them into our world—the world of the classroom and academia. This is especially important when we are asking students to learn through risk and uncertainty. Students want and need to know that someone cares about them, that their well-being will be looked after, and that there are support structures built into the class. Starting with their world means investing in relationship building in the class. Much more than simply knowing everyone's names, real relationship building means thinking of your students as a learning community. Who are they? What are their lives like? What are they nervous about? Why are they here? One simple tool to start in their world is the student information sheet. Every class I have taught in the last 10 years begins with this assignment. On day one, I ask every student to complete the student information sheet and download it to the learning management system. The sheet asks for their name and preferred gender pronouns, their major (if decided), and any outside activity they are involved in and the approximate hours spent per week on them (things like athletics, work-study, volunteering, family requirements, etc.). The form asks them to list what other courses they are taking that semester and the total number of credits. Finally, I ask a few more narrative questions: "What are your expectations for this class?" And, "What do I need to know about you to best support you and your learning this semester?" This exercise has always paid huge dividends for me. I get to know my students at a deeper level, and they often share surprisingly candid reflections. Students have told me things like, "I am shy and don't always speak up but if you call on me, it will help me participate more." Or, "My brother was in a bad car accident this summer and I go home on weekends to help support him and my family." I often refer to the compiled and printed out inventories as I move through the semester. It helps me memorize names and personalize my feedback and work with each student.

Once we get into their world, our job is to create a sense of our world—the world where student interests and lived experiences interact with course content, goals, and objectives. Importantly, the "ours" in the Theirs-Ours-Theirs model is not the instructor's world—it is the world jointly created by the students and the instructor *together*. How can we build a shared sense of the enterprise? How do we create a community of learning? We will discuss this specifically in the Bow and the Arrow concept that follows. Before we move on, however, the Theirs-Ours-Theirs model has one more stage. The final "theirs" refers to how we facilitate reflection and connections for students as they conclude a class period, unit, or course. If we have started in their world and then co-created an our world, we must finally help them make connections and integrations back into their world—whether that involves personal insights, academic connections to other classes and content, or integrations into life beyond college (career and vocational discernment, for example). We are learning more and more about the importance of metacognition and integrative learning. The move back into the students' world is all about helping them think about their learning in more purposeful and deliberate ways. This is especially important while facilitating appropriate risk-taking and learning for uncertainty. Students who are in a state of uncertainty often worry that they aren't learning or that they may be doing it wrong. Building opportunities for reflection and for metacognition allows students to capture their learning in more overt ways. For example, when I advised students who had just come back from a semester studying abroad, I would often ask them how it went. "It was great," they would say and then follow that up with a story or two. "What new knowledge, skills, or aptitudes did you gain that you think you could list on your resume?" I would ask. This question was usually met with silence. Students often struggle to make the connection between their experience and usefulness in this sense. I would often help them make connections by asking things like, "What about the internship you completed? Do you think you learned new skills from that experience?" Or, "In what ways have you broadened your intercultural competencies as a result of your semester abroad?" Asking these sorts of questions helps students "make the invisible, visible" by directly connecting the experience to their lives and their future.

THE BOW AND THE ARROW

I forget who first introduced me to this concept, but it has stuck with me for years and I often bring it up in workshops. The Bow and the Arrow concept is about return on investment. When we think about the process of shooting an arrow, almost all of the time, focus, and energy are in pulling back the bow with the arrow attached. But, when we think about it, this is actually taking the arrow in the *opposite* direction of where we want it to go. However, that investment in time, attention, and energy in going "backwards" pays huge dividends when we finally release the arrow. In essence, the more work we do pulling backward, the farther the arrow goes forward. In terms of facilitating risk and uncertainty, the Bow and the Arrow means taking time to build relationships and a sense of community in the learning environment. In addition to starting in the students' world, the Bow and the Arrow concept suggests that we dedicate *more* time to things like group norms, classroom routines, expectations, and tone setting. I typically reserve at least two classes at the beginning of the semester for students to get to know each other and me. We often refer to these as "ice breaker" activities and exercises, but this doesn't quite get at the idea. We don't want to facilitate a disconnected series of awkward and sometimes jarring "games" for a few classes and then leave it all behind as we officially start the course. Rather, the Bow and the Arrow concept suggests that we think about relationship building and facilitating a sense of classroom community *throughout* the semester. An exercise I often use at the beginning of classes is taken from a tool used on many Outward Bound courses called the "Full Value Contract." This exercise involves asking students to think about what they will do individually and what they want the class to do collectively in order to get the "full value" out of the experience. A list is generated and discussed with the faculty member facilitating. Once the class is happy with the stated principles, expectations, and values, the list becomes a "contract" for the class. I often print it out and make sure everyone has a copy. Sometimes, we create a poster that hangs on the wall as a reminder. Periodically, we check back in on the contract to see how we are doing and whether or not the stated expectations and values need reconsidering.

In addition to the beginning of the semester exercises, I often have several moments during a semester when we pause the classroom content. For example, about one month in, I will do an exercise called "Continue-Start-Stop" where I ask students to anonymously complete cards that they turn in to me answering the following questions: What should we continue to do in this class that is working? What should we start doing as a class that we have not yet? What should we stop doing that is not working? I compile and organize the results thematically and then I present them during the next class. There is often a range of feedback—some more useful than others—but it gives the students a window into my world as the instructor and opens up the space for a conversation about how things are going and what might be adjusted.

At this point a reader may wonder and worry that all this emphasis on relationships and facilitating classroom community is time intensive and takes away from classroom content. First, doing things like this throughout the semester takes less time than you may think; 15 minutes of time dedicated to community building sprinkled throughout a semester is typically not a huge time burden. And, it is worth noting that the return on that investment (the bow and the arrow) is students who are more comfortable with each other and you which allows them to take more appropriate risks and perform at their best—outcomes we are "shooting" for. The bow flies farther.

THE BOILED FROG

Many folks have heard the old saw about the frog and the boiling water. In case you haven't, it goes something like this: If you try to put a frog in boiling water, it will very much refuse, or if placed in it, it will try desperately to jump out. However, if you put a frog in lukewarm water and then slowly turn up the heat, it won't notice the changes and it "adapts." Leaving aside the rather gruesome analogy here, the Boiling Frog concept can help us as we think about facilitating for uncertainty in teaching and learning. At the core of this idea is the notion of gradient and progression in learning. When a student (or anyone) perceives a risky environment or situation, there are specific responses that occur physiologically. Often referred to as "flight or fight," the brain can perceive risk as a threat and respond in ways that are not helpful at all for facilitating learning (MacLean, 1978). We often think of "stress" as an inherently bad condition. However, the neuroscience of stress suggests that there are actually two kinds of stress: "eustress" or good stress and "distress" or bad stress. The physiological responses to these two very different forms of stress are pronounced. When we perceive risk as "eustress," we approach the learning situation in a state of engagement, excitement, and general positivity. For example, a student who has had practice presenting their research in front of the class multiple times is then asked to present at a regional conference. While that student may still be nervous, it is a good kind of nervous and they approach the challenge with a heightened sense of engagement and awareness. The brain response is to activate our higher order thinking skills. The experience, while stressful, results in a heightened sense of self-efficacy and confidence for that student. In contrast to eustress, when we experience distress, we approach a learning situation in something closer to panic. Cortisol is released, which acts as a neuroinhibitor, and the amygdala, that area of our brain that creates a flight or fight response, is heightened and activated. To go back to our public speaking example, students who have no preparation and no practice and are suddenly thrust into a public speaking role in front of strangers might "freeze" on stage or stumble their way through a presentation. The heart is racing too fast, the face is flushed, and the breathing rate is too high. They may survive it, but the experience may leave them with a significant lack of confidence and may color their willingness or ability to speak in public in the future.

So how do we refrain from boiling our students in uncertain learning situations? Practice, practice, practice. Relatively low-stakes practice is one of the best ways to get students comfortable being uncomfortable. We do this when we have our students do a paired share, first with another student before then asking the class as a whole to offer their thoughts on a given question or topic. The paired share is low-stakes practice. It allows students to, when called upon, say "well, *we* thought. . . ." The student may still feel stress, but hopefully it is eustress and leads to heightened engagement and a willingness to try new challenges. A job-shadowing experience is a useful low-stakes practice in advance of a summer internship. A writing assignment that is required to go through multiple drafts is another form of low-stakes practice. Interviewing a friend first before interviewing a stranger for a community oral history project assignment gives students a trial run and an invitation to take further risks. The point in facilitating uncertain learning environments is that we don't actually want to remove all stress and make the environment "safe" for students. In this definition of safe, what we have created is boredom and disengagement. We want to actively facilitate a kind of stress that students perceive as a challenge—something to engage with and to bring their best selves to the learning.

III. COMMON TRAPS IN RISKY TEACHING

In facilitating faculty workshops on risky teaching, I have found that, in addition to introducing the idea of a playlist of useful tools and concepts, it is equally important to talk, overtly, about common mistakes, traps, and things to avoid. Perhaps this is the metaphorical equivalent of jamming out to a great series of songs on the playlist only to find out that someone has inserted "We Built This City" by Starship on there.[3] That stuff just needs to be deleted or it will ruin the whole vibe. So, with that, here are the most common traps and things to avoid as you consider designing your teaching and learning to include more risk and uncertainty.

RELEVANCE, CHALLENGE, AND INTEGRATION

During one of my visits to a campus, a faculty member approached me after my workshop with a question. "I am very experiential with my classes," she remarked, "but my students don't seem very engaged when I create these kinds of opportunities. How can I get them to buy-in to what I am asking them to do?" I asked her to give me an example of one of her experiential assignments, and she described a counseling psychology course where students were asked to spend time throughout the semester at a local animal shelter with a class partner and play with the animals there. She billed it as a combination of service learning and practical skill development for the students. The assigned work was a written journal. Curious as to the connections between the animal shelter and counseling, I asked her to say more about how she saw that assignment as relevant to the course and the learning outcomes. "Well," she said, "I wanted them to work together and to interact and observe behavior as this is a fundamental aspect of counseling." The more we talked, the more it became clear that one of the reasons the students were not very engaged with the assignment was a lack of perceived relevance. The instructor had, for good reasons, decided on the animal shelter option because having students involved in "real" counseling settings with people has obvious ethical challenges. But, in an effort to have her students do something experiential and fulfill a service learning course designation, this faculty member had fallen into several traps. By not effectively connecting the activity to the learning goals of the course, she had emphasized activity at the expense of relevant learning. By simply asking them to play with the animals and record their observations, there was insufficient uncertainty or risk associated with the activities. To use Boiling Frog, the water never got hot enough. Students trudged out to the shelter on a weekly basis and played with the animals. Their journal reflections were, unsurprisingly, shallow and vacuous. It was not really a surprise that students questioned the value of the exercise and put little effort into it.

How can we ensure that we don't fall into the irrelevance trap when designing and facilitating for risk and uncertainty in learning? First, go back to first principles with the course and the learning objectives. Make sure to clearly connect and integrate learning outcomes and goals with any assignments and activities using backwards design or the integrated model from Fink. Second, make sure that there is something at stake with the exercise. Remember your BMAG. Design the course and/or the assignment in a way that students will know that doing the work will matter beyond just the grade. In our example with the counseling psychology course, perhaps students could research pet therapy as a topic and engage with the animal shelter to imagine ways in which the nonprofit organization could offer pet therapy options in the community as a way to get the pets out in public, increase their publicity, and provide a service? Perhaps the students could then present the results of their work to the leadership of the animal shelter at the end of the semester? Third, offer students choice. No one much likes being told what to do. Students generally accept traditional classroom assignments as something they must do. But when we move out into nontraditional assignments and activities, their skepticism can increase. By providing them with choices about how to design and complete these assignments, you have a better chance of increasing their overall engagement. In our example with counseling psychology, the instructor could offer several different types of service learning and community engagement and let students self-select what area they are most interested in exploring. Fourth, make sure there is sufficient challenge associated with the activity. That challenge could be content-driven, intrapersonal, interpersonal, or some combination of the three. As we have discussed, students may perceive risk and uncertainty differently, so, ideally, you would add in flexibility and differentiation through choice. Finally, frequent, iterative feedback helps students stay on track and ensures that your desired learning outcomes stay visible and integrated into the activity and assignment.

TIME MANAGEMENT, ASSESSMENT, AND GRADING

In addition to the issues associated with relevance, challenge, and integration, another common trap in designing and facilitating uncertainty and risk in learning has to do with time management. Early on in my career, I had the idea of asking my students to produce a "zine" (an informal magazine meant for public distribution) for the local community around the topics we were exploring in class. I had the relevance, challenge, and integration issues addressed, and the students were excited to learn about the project at the beginning of the semester and interested to give it a go. My fatal mistake was that I viewed the project and assignment as a sort of final exam. In the final exam paradigm, we pile in as much content as possible throughout the semester, and then, at the end, we ask students to demonstrate, in a condensed period of time, that they now understand all that content. In this case, we worked through environmental history and theory for the first 12 weeks. Then, I broke them into groups and with three weeks left in the semester said, "Now go out and produce your zines"! The problems materialized instantly. Some groups had a hard time getting started. Others got started but immediately bogged down in arranging the interviews they wanted to do in the community. They *all* struggled mightily with formatting and page layout issues (it turns out that laying out a magazine from a pagination standpoint is more complicated than it first appears). While the students were game, it was clear I had not planned well enough. By exam week, we were all scrambling trying to get the zines printed and distributed. The end result was ok, but far less than what I had hoped for and envisioned. The following year, I re-did the assignment with time management as a key design element.

When we move off the tried and true (tired and blue?) structure of midterm and final exams, both students and instructors need to think of themselves as project managers. Most risky and uncertain learning requires project management. How can we effectively design and facilitate projects that promote productive risk and uncertainty? In the second iteration of my zine assignment, I scaffolded the activity over the course of the entire semester. Early on, I introduced the concept and talked about the learning goals and expectations. I also showed them some exemplars and described how and why they were effective. Then, I broke students into groups to brainstorm possible ideas and structures. I scheduled an early check-in point for students to submit a project proposal document that I graded and provided feedback on using a rubric I developed. I had a librarian come talk to the class about printing and layout software that could be used to produce the zines. Two thirds of the way through the semester, I had the student groups present on their drafts and progress in peer feedback sessions, as well as in front of the class as a whole. Finally, I left time at the end of the semester for the class to come together to see the finished products and provide additional peer feedback as well as individual reflections on the project as a whole. The second version of my zine assignment was substantially better—both in terms of the student experience and in terms of the final products and learning outcomes.

I have learned, since that early failure, to "chunk" uncertain and risky assignments. I provide more progress check-ins and integrate graded feedback along the way to help keep everything on track. I also learned that these are great opportunities to incorporate peer review and to develop (and heighten) class expectations regarding quality. Finally, by managing the time and the project throughout the semester, my students can put more care, thought, and effort into the final product. This prevents "cramming" and the inevitable poor results that come from it. And, by finishing before the end of the semester, I can provide opportunities for reflection and group processing of the assignment and the class as a whole.

CONCLUSION

When I think back to what made Armen's concrete lab experiment so effective, I see the intentional incorporation of many of the elements we have explored in this chapter. Armen shifted the design to put the experience before the label, ensuring that students were immersed in messy, uncertain problem solving first and then were given opportunities to further their learning and try again. The assignment structure was relevant and timely, and it gave the students a real-world connection to what they were studying in the course and an opportunity to apply what they were learning in meaningful ways. The lab activities were challenging and involved elements of risk and uncertainty—avoiding a cookbook design structure that simply asked them to follow scripted instructions and processes. And yet, many of these changes and adjustments were not revolutionary. They were relatively small and easy to incorporate, but had a significant return on investment (small teaching). Designing and facilitating for uncertainty need not require a complete overhaul of your course or syllabus. Like the Boiling Frog, you can start out lukewarm and try to incorporate a relatively minor change. For me, once I saw and experienced the increased engagement from my students and the improved learning outcomes, I was hooked. It may start out with small changes, but, fair warning, it can be hard to go back once you get started. Author Elizabeth Appell (1979) once wrote, "And the day came when the risk to remain tight in the bud was more painful than the risk it took to blossom."[4] This reminds us that staying put to avoid change is *also* a risk. But risky teaching doesn't have to be painful. Like a flower moving from bud to bloom, we can view it as a process of slow, steady unfolding rather than some sudden and dramatic shift. Each of us can enter into that process of unfolding in our own way. For some, it may be an experiment with project-based learning. For others, it may be trying out a flipped classroom or a new active learning method. There are as many ways to work with risk and uncertainty in the classroom as there are flowers in the field. And the goal is to let them all bloom.

NOTES

1. For more on the Learning in Action program, see http://learninginaction.ua.edu/
2. See David Gooblar (2019), "Is it ever ok to lecture?" www.chronicle.com/article/Is-It-Ever-OK-to/245458
3. The 2011 *Rolling Stone* magazine readers' poll named this song the worst song of the 1980s by the largest margin in the history of the poll. Retrieved from: www.rollingstone.com/music/music-lists/readers-poll-the-10-worst-songs-of-the-1980s-20488/1-starship-we-built-this-city-17392/
4. This quotation is often misattributed on the internet to poet Anaïs Nin. While still in some dispute, the evidence suggests Elizabeth Appell as the original author. See here for more information: http://anaisninblog.skybluepress.com/2013/03/who-wrote-risk-is-the-mystery-solved/

REFERENCES

Appell, E. (1979). *No title*. Orinda, CA: John F. Kennedy University.

Fink, D. L. (2005). *Integrated course design*. Manhattan, KS: The IDEA Center.

Gooblar, D. (2019). *Is it ever ok to lecture?* Retrieved from: www.chronicle.com/article/is-it-ever-ok-to-lecture/

Lang, J. M. (2016). *Small teaching: Everyday lessons from the science of learning*. New York: John Wiley & Sons.

MacLean, P. D. (1978). A mind of three minds: Educating the triune brain. In *Education and the brain* (pp. 308–342). Chicago, IL: National Society for the Study of Education.

Prince, M. (2004). Does active learning work? A review of the research. *Journal of Engineering Education*, 93(3), 223–231.

Wiggins, G. P., & McTighe, J. (2005). *Understanding by design*. Alexandria, VA: Association for Supervision and Curriculum Development.

Chapter 6
Uncertainty Beyond the Classroom

INTRODUCTION

Teaching and learning outside the traditional four walls of the classroom is risky. For many of us, the classroom *is* where teaching and learning happens. During the early days of the Covid-19 crisis, I was speaking to a friend and colleague of mine working at a university an international university. When the administration decided to close down the campus and send the students home, like faculty everywhere, the faculty at this university scrambled to transition their courses to an online format. My colleague recalled seeing instructors show up on campus to teach at their prescribed time in their prescribed lecture hall. They would stand at the lectern and record their lecture to a theater of empty seats. Apparently, so many faculty wanted to record their lectures in in this manner that the university finally had to disallow the practice. Such is the pull of the classroom; even when there are no students in it, and when the campus is effectively closed, we are drawn to the comfort, the familiarity, and the routine of the space.

As a different example, my daughter's pre-Covid high school experience involved almost no time outside of the school or the classroom. In two years, she spent a total of *three days* with her teachers in classes that actually left the school building. In one case (a biology class), it was to walk outside for 10 minutes to look at a particular species of tree. In another, it was a field trip (also biology) to a local natural area to help band birds on a Saturday. But besides these forays, her entire formal learning in high school has been inside, in a classroom. And we do, after all, teach as we are taught. Indoor classrooms are a near cultural universal. Visit any country and almost any modern educational system, and the physical structure and organization of the school will look very familiar. We learn in rooms (almost always square-shaped), separated out and connected by hallways. This, of course, is a vestige of our industrial age and the fact that the modern educational system in the United States and in other parts of the world emerged in the late 19th and early 20th centuries around the same time that our modern industrialized

DOI: 10.4324/9781003029809-8

economy emerged. The one-room schoolhouse was replaced by larger structures modeled after the mass production systems and organizational efficiency of the factory. And it was by necessity: In order to educate more children and a growing urbanized population, progressive educators at the time organized a system built around efficiency. The bells, periods, separated classrooms, and masses of students moving through the hallways that we take for granted today emerged directly from the shift changes and efficient organization of workers in the industrialized factories of the early 20th century in the United States and in other parts of the world. This way of placing learning inside the four-walled classroom is now so taken for granted it is difficult to imagine other forms and locations of teaching and learning. The teachers in my daughter's high school would probably tell you that they *want* to do more teaching outside the classroom, but it is simply not possible given the organization of the school day, the number of students they must teach, the timing of classes in 55-minute periods, the lack of transportation options, and the associated legal complexities. Despite these hurdles, some schools do manage to engage the wider community through learning outside the classroom. Place-based education, service learning, and community-based learning are all recognized methodologies in primary and secondary education. Expeditionary Learning Schools, forest schools, and Big Picture schools are just several examples of programs and curricula that demonstrate that learning outside the formal classroom is both possible and effective.

It is perhaps a little easier for us in higher education to get around some of the challenges associated with leaving the classroom, but not entirely so. For some disciplines, there is a built-in field experience component of the curriculum that expands the learning outside the lecture hall—practicums, required internships and work experiences, and field trips, for example. There are even entire curriculums and four-year plans organized around out-of-class experiences. The "co-op" model, popularized by schools such as the University of Cincinnati and Northeastern University, typically involves students spending at least a summer or a semester embedded in an internship or work-integrated experience. There are schools that require community engagement as part of the four-year degree and weave it into graduation requirements. For example, Warren Wilson College, where I currently work, requires students to complete a scaffolded set of three community-engaged experiences, ending with a signature experience in the junior or senior year involving sustained and significant engagement and a project with a local or regional community partner. Besides these institution-wide approaches, there are also faculty, across the disciplines, who leave the classroom behind and take their students (and often their scholarship) into the community. History students are using a geographic information system (GIS) to map forgotten pre–civil rights era Black churches in Alabama based on oral history research. Biology students are cataloguing threatened plant species in a proposed new state park. English students are organizing Shakespeare festivals in conjunction with city planners. Computer science students are using modeling software to plan more efficient public transportation routes in rural communities. "Public" scholarship and pedagogy of this sort are growing across all types of institutions in higher education—from community colleges and regional publics to national liberal arts schools and flagship state universities. Institutions, both public and private, increasingly see the need and opportunity to align their mission with the needs and challenges of the local community. These out-of-classroom opportunities can demonstrate, in a tangible and visible way, the benefits of higher education to a somewhat skeptical public. They can also help strengthen town-gown relationships in communities where the relationship between the college and the community can be somewhat strained. This work can also be critical to gaining additional funding—something presidents, provosts, and boards are always interested in. Yet, despite these benefits, many faculty find it difficult to take the risk of moving teaching and learning outside the classroom. The issues and challenges here are some of the same that arise when we talk about taking risks *inside* the classroom: "It takes too much time." "My discipline is not well suited to it." "It seems too complicated." "What would I actually *do* with students?" When these questions and issues come up, I often tell a story about Mike.

CHEMISTRY IN THE COMMUNITY

Mike Deibel is a professor of chemistry at Earlham College. I have known Mike for over 20 years, and he is, in many ways, a model and example of how we grow into risky teaching. When I first arrived at Earlham, Mike, by his own admission, was a pretty traditional professor. He saw his work with his students as almost entirely centered around lectures and labs, completed in the natural science building on campus. But Mike noted that his field, analytical chemistry, actually deals with the concept of uncertainty quite often. When I spoke with him while doing research for this book, he noted,

> For those of us in the analytical chemistry world, uncertainty is something you live with all the time and it's a core concept. . . . One of the things we stress with our students is about how well you actually know a number. You can use something as simple as the nutrition information on a package and realize that the number listed is not as certain as it seems. There is always a plus or minus around it.

One year, Mike helped organize an interdisciplinary science research program funded by the Keck Foundation that involved every department in the science division at that time. The grant project was designed to give students and faculty opportunities to complete real-world, interdisciplinary research, both in and out of the lab. One of the projects involved taking students out to a local lake to study lakebed sediment given that this area is located in an area of historic contamination from a former industrial site. When he talked about this experience, he recalled how amazed he was at the engagement of the students on this project. "One of the things I found most fascinating that was more eye opening than maybe it should have been was how turned on students got when they went outside." Mike continued,

> This was a group of Math, Computer Science, and chemistry students literally dragging a bunch of sensors behind canoes in the middle of this unremarkable lake in the summer. We did GIS mapping and core sampling by taking out these tiny little plugs from the bottom of the lake. . . . It was amazing to see how energized the students were from that day and the kind of conversations they were having amongst themselves.

Mike was impressed, and the project expanded to include more students from more classes.

> The trickle down was that we kept making mini trips bringing groups of students from classes and they would do real sampling of real things and bring them back to the lab to add to the dataset so they could see that they were building this scientific body of knowledge that would be useful for the community.

It was such a simple activity, taking students out to the local lake in a canoe to gather samples to be analyzed back in the lab. But there was something in the kind of engagement and learning Mike saw from the students that had him intrigued.

> That first Keck project led to the acquisition of an instrument that we used to start a project in Chile analyzing pottery—and we took students along with us to do that. That led to another trip, this time to China, to do more pottery analyses there.

One thing led to another, and Mike, Corrine (Mike's wife and also a chemistry professor at Earlham), and their students analyzed everything from kombucha from a small, local, food production farm to an Egyptian mummy in a regional history museum and archeological artifacts around the world.

This is often how it starts in my experience. A faculty member just gives it a go—starting with something small and venturing out of the classroom with students as an experiment or trial. Often, but not always, faculty come back from such experiences inspired to try more. They see the difference it makes for students to be outside the traditional four walls and engaged with the content in a different (and often more immediately relevant) way. And, once they go, they see that it's not so bad and that they can try other forms of out-of-class teaching and learning.

The time commitments and structure expand, and some even start designing their entire course around learning outside the classroom. In Mike's case, from his initial foray in a canoe on the local lake, he expanded his chemistry in the community to a host of out-of-classroom experiences. Mike and Corinne have since led multiple off-campus study programs to France, New Zealand, and Peru. And recently, Mike organized and implemented a ground-breaking, innovative interdisciplinary public health course with faculty from across the college at Earlham, including the humanities, social sciences, and natural sciences, working with health-care professionals in a bilingual medical setting in Indianapolis. The students spent two weeks in the classroom with faculty from a range of disciplines learning everything from Spanish, to intercultural competency, to public health, and they then applied that knowledge by being fully immersed in a bilingual health-care setting practicing specific skills like checking blood pressures and taking medical histories. To Mike, the benefits of this work far outweigh the challenges.

> Taking chances and risks like this will lead you to places you would never suspect you would go. That's what makes it worth it. And, it will lead students to go to places they never thought they would go. You will watch your students put in more time, more effort, and be more engaged.

All of this began from a small nudge and a simple step of taking students outside the classroom. I chose to feature Mike's story because, as a professor of chemistry, he teaches in a highly sequenced, content-heavy, accredited discipline with strict requirements about what must be taught and in what order. Often, faculty will say that they are intrigued by or interested in learning outside the classroom, but that their discipline, their major, or their course requirements simply do not allow it. Sometimes this may be true. But much more often, I find that we build our own iron cages. The four-walled classroom is one we construct with our minds, and it is one we can expand and move beyond if we want. If a professor of chemistry can do it, you can do it, too.

As I write this, thousands of faculty across higher education are teaching from their homes, having had to transition to online distance learning as a result of the Covid-19 crisis. It took a global pandemic to force many of us to experiment with and attempt online learning. What we are doing is most decidedly *not* best-in-class distance learning, and many of us will gladly trade the Zoom videoconferencing awkwardness and LMS discussion forums for our regular, in-person classrooms just as soon as we can. But, one silver lining from this experience is the realization that we *can*, in fact, change and embrace new approaches—even if in this case it was forced upon many of us. We may not stay with an entirely online learning modality, but our eyes have been opened to new possibilities and new ways of enhancing the teaching and learning experience. The talk now of our "new normal" in higher education is all about hybridity and the blending of in-person and online learning. The same could be true for learning in the community. Learning outside the classroom *is* possible. And you might be surprised at the myriad ways it can occur.

COMMUNITIES AS CLASSROOMS

Out-of-class teaching and learning experiences take on a number of different forms, names, and approaches, including the following.

Practicums	Off-campus or international study
Field trips	Service learning
Internships	Place-based learning
Externships	Community-based research

While many definitions exist and there is significant variability in the methods, they all center on the idea that significant learning can take place outside the classroom and in the community (whether defined as the campus, the local region, or further afield). While most of these approaches involve groups of students formally organized around a course or class project, there is also learning happening outside the classroom in the form of internships and practicums that students may experience individually. Study abroad, study away, and off-campus study programs and experiences also, to varying degrees, involve learning outside the classroom. Finally, informal learning through the co-curriculum has always been recognized on residential campuses as an important part of a student's development and undergraduate career. Each of these approaches aims to situate learning "in place" and draw from the specific geography, history, ecology, and/or culture of that place to facilitate learning. The best forms of community-engaged learning integrate concepts of reciprocity and community capacity building into the engagement. That is, ensuring that any learning that happens in external places occurs in ways that don't just benefit the students or the university but also benefit the local community in tangible ways through careful collaboration and partnership (Sobania, 2015).

In addition to extending learning beyond the campus boundaries, we must not forget the many ways students can learn outside the classroom while remaining on campus. Our colleagues in student and residential life have long known about the potential power of learning outside of the classroom. Overlooked areas of campus experiences like work-study programs and student club leadership can be and have been used for things like campus-wide education initiatives, on-campus internships, and, given the current Covid-19 challenges, student health ambassadorships. A look within your own campus can yield a surprising variety of opportunities to engage students in learning outside the classroom. One example of this form of on-campus, out-of-classroom learning was a creative and highly effective "alternative campus tour" designed by an American studies class at a flagship state university, which I had the privilege to observe several years ago. The professor for the class was somewhat frustrated by the standard admissions tour that left out some of the more difficult moments in the history of the university, especially during the civil rights era, and she wanted to design a class project that involved learning outside of the classroom in some manner. So, she worked with her class to design an alternative tour—one that visited locations and places on campus where significant moments of conflict had occurred during the fight for civil rights. Over the course of the semester, the students completed local research on the history of the civil rights struggle on their campus. They then compiled that information and designed an alternative campus tour that visited sites of significance around campus and detailed the untold history of the school during that time. I had the opportunity to attend this tour and watched as the students presented their research; I left extremely impressed—by their engagement, by the quality of their research, and by the fact that the class setting was now the campus as a whole. It was such a hit that the tour carried on after that initial class—though it was, to my knowledge, never fully sanctioned by the university. Taking the learning out of the classroom can often challenge the status quo in uncomfortable ways. David Gruenwald noted, "Once one begins to appreciate the pedagogical power of places, it is difficult to accept institutional discourses, structures, pedagogies, and curriculums that neglect them" (2003b, p. 641).

For too long, many college campuses have existed as "Universities of Nowhere." It is as if the teaching and learning that go on in these places could happen anywhere—that the actual place, its history, its geography, its culture, and its people have no bearing on knowledge construction and acquisition. If we ignore our places, learning becomes decontextualized—something that should give us pause when we consider the moral and ethical consequences of knowledge attainment. Yet, the barriers and obstacles involved in leaving the classroom are real. Designing these experiences for students requires a different set of skills, tools, and methods than what is typically needed in the traditional classroom. It also involves a fair amount of uncertainty—both for the student and the instructor. It can be risky. So, why try it?

A DESERT EPIPHANY

In 2003, I led an off-campus study semester called Southwest Field Studies (SWFS). The ultimate field-based program, SWFS spent four months in the deserts of the American Southwest and Mexico with a focus on interdisciplinary environmental studies. Our classroom was the desert and the diverse communities that inhabit this region of the world—from big cities like Tucson and Phoenix to remote areas of the Sonoran and Chihuahuan Deserts. We traveled in two,

15-passenger vans—one towing a trailer full of our gear and one tricked out with a mobile library. This was a time before Wi-Fi and the smartphone, so we relied on a collection of field guides and books on the natural history of the area in addition to local experts to help us learn about the regions and make sense of the myriad issues—from water conflicts, to immigration issues, to conservation biology, to Indigenous rights. That year, we had planned to spend a three-week unit on Indigenous Ecological Knowledge Systems by visiting with and learning from the Seri (Comcáac) people of northwestern Mexico. Anthropologists Gary Nabhan and Lori Monti, a husband and wife team, had worked with the Seri for many years, and we were lucky enough to have the opportunity to join Dr. Monti on this particular trip.

Leading up to the semester, one of my students, Melanie,[1] who was majoring in anthropology, knew we would be visiting with the Seri community in Desemboque, Mexico, and was convinced that this would be the highlight of the semester for her. In many ways, it was the entire reason she elected to sign up for the program in the first place. Melanie was fascinated with the study of Indigenous cultures, and, as a sophomore, she anticipated focusing her career on Native American causes and issues in the United States. Our schedule put us in Mexico visiting with the Seri in mid-February, and she was somewhat impatient to get to that part of the course and semester. It was clear to her that this experience would be transformative. And it was. Just not in the ways she thought.

The road into Desemboque at that time was not for the faint of heart. You leave the last major town, Kino Bay, and travel down a dirt and gravel road for over three hours. The scenery is breathtaking—the Sea of Cortez stretches out before you popping in azure blue contrast against the more muted grays, browns, and greens of the desert floor. Large cardon cacti stand like lonely sentinels along the rocky hilltops and mountains, lending a sense of solitude and emptiness to the landscape. It would be majestic if it weren't for the road. And "road" was a bit of an overstatement. It was a washboard-like, rutted, boulder-strewn obstacle course that required you as the driver to choose between two undesirable options—drive fast to avoid the horrific vibrations that came from the washboard road but risk losing control of the van, or drive slow for safety and endure three hours in a jackhammer with wheels. In the end, we chose the slow option, and it made for a long, uncomfortable journey into Desemboque.

Halfway down the road, we stopped for a break and to do some roadside herpetology with one of our faculty experts. We headed down a wash in search of lizards, geckos, and whatever else we could find and spent a joyous couple of hours wandering around. As we headed back to the vans, I was trailing behind and noticed several students peering curiously at our trailer. As I got closer, I could tell why. The trailer tires were flat. All of them. "That's strange," I said. Then I had my first realization—we only had one spare tire for the trailer. That led to my second realization—this was no accident. "Someone purposefully slashed the tires,"

UNCERTAINTY BEYOND THE CLASSROOM

I said. "But why would someone do that?" a student replied. "That's just mean—now we can't go anywhere." "I think that's the point," I replied back. Everything we needed was in that trailer—tents, sleeping bags, food, equipment, and clothes. We couldn't abandon it. By slashing all four tires, our local vandals left us sitting ducks—two hours down a dirt road in the middle of the Sonoran Desert with a sea to our west and a mountain range to our east. Nowhere to go. As the enormity of the situation increasingly dawned on us, we needed a plan.

I had signed up to lead a four-month field study, sure, but I was pretty sure I had not signed up for *this*. Some students began crying and others just looked stunned. As faculty, the classroom and the laboratory are our domains. We can (mostly) control those environments, and, even when we can't, we have an "out." Classes and labs have a time limit. There is no time limit on off-campus study. And, you can't just call campus safety or student life when there is a problem. While there are many, many benefits in my mind to taking students out of the classroom and into the community, it *does* come with risks—sometimes quite literal ones. In this case, my mind was swirling with emotions. What should we do? What *could* we do? I don't know how to respond to this. This is not part of my training or experience. Then I remembered something I had read from a book on spiritual meditation—when experiencing a struggle, a crisis, or chaos, your entire being will want to speed up. But that is precisely when it is important to *slow down*. We gathered our group together in a circle, and I talked about the situation, about how it felt, and about what our plans were. Then I asked that we spend some time in silence. As students and faculty working at a Quaker college, a moment of silence is a common practice and a comforting ritual for our group. As we sat on the desert floor in silence, I quietly prayed for my own salvation as the leader who had got us into this mess. Thankfully, I was not alone, and between my wife, Bill, my biologist colleague, and our teaching assistant (TA), we hatched a plan. Our TA and Bill would drive the vans the rest of the way into Desemboque to get help from the village. The rest of us would wait it out by the trailer, hoping that our sheer numbers would protect us from vandals. If we did see a car coming, the students were told to scatter into the desert to hide. It was a long two-hour wait. Just as the sun was setting, we saw headlights emerge from the direction of Desemboque. Still unsure as to who it was, we instructed the students to scatter. My wife and I looked at each other and stood as confidently as we could waiting for our fate. Finally, we could make out the vehicle and were relieved to see our trusty maroon college vans approaching. And behind them, a rusty, white pickup truck filled with tires of all shapes and sizes. And, just to add extra drama to the whole scene, two men in the back of the pickup were holding guns. Never was a Quaker so happy to see a man with a gun!

The local villagers jimmy-rigged their spare tires onto our trailer, and we drove off, caravan-style, towing a rickety trailer with an armed escort. Because we could not drive the trailer fast, we arrived in Desemboque after dark. As a remote village well off the supply line for state services, the small community of Desemboque had no electricity at that time. This was not how I had envisioned introducing my students to the community—something I knew would have involved culture shock in the best of circumstances. But, as the saying goes, "adventure is what happens when things don't go according to plan," and we were certainly having an adventure. The Comcáac had lit a large bonfire around a central, communal building, and we arrived to dancing, singing, and warm greetings. We sat around the fire and even joined in some of the dancing—the Comcáac have a specific dance they do involving lots of stomping and kicking on a wooden platform (traditionally, they would have done this on the back of a turtle shell). It was a memorable evening, and I relaxed, confident we had navigated the worst of it.

The next morning, as I wormed my way out of my sleeping bag and went in search of breakfast, I saw a student out of the corner of my eye sitting by herself and crying. It was Melanie. I went to sit next to her. "What's up?" I asked, certain I would hear her talk about the trauma of the trailer tire slashing vandals. "Why do they kick their dogs!?" she cried. The night before, around the bonfire, many of the local village dogs were slinking about trying to beg for scraps of food. These were not pets in the same way we might think of them in the United States. They were skinny, mangy, and sad looking, and, when they got too close, many Comcáac would give them a good, swift kick to shoo them away. The dogs would invariably give out a loud whelp and move away until they built up enough courage to try again. To Melanie, this was animal abuse, and it shocked her to see people that she was so interested in learning about and from do something so contrary to her values. "It's wrong!" she cried angrily. As I tried to help her come to grips with her culture shock, it was clear that Melanie's preconceived notions about the Comcáac were not fitting the reality on the ground. Where were the famed "Indigenous environmentalists" she had heard so much about? All she could see around her were cinder block homes, trash blowing around the dusty streets, and roving packs of skinny, abused dogs.

One of the reasons off-campus study can be considered a high-impact practice for students is because of the ways in which it can create unexpected situations. Richard Kraft (1992) called these "strange-land experiences" and discussed how such experiences can reorient thinking, values, and behavior. Designed well, such experiences can make the strange, familiar and the familiar, strange. Wrestling with uncertainty and with situations and experiences that do not go according to plan can invite deeper thinking about not only academic subject matter but also about personal values, attitudes, and beliefs. This type of holistic or integrated learning is often at the center of powerful and transformative experiences in college. The research on high-impact practices (Kuh, 2008) indicates that learning experiences such as study away and service learning are some of the most significant for students. In Melanie's case, her time in Desemboque was an intense experience—something that would greatly influence her sense of vocational discernment. She never completely got over her issue with how Comcáac people treated their dogs, but she did reconcile some of her previous notions of what it meant to be an environmentalist with what she saw and experienced on the ground in the village. Her previous, somewhat romanticized conceptions became more complex and nuanced. And, her reflections on why she was so upset about the dogs led her to another realization—animal rights was a real passion of hers, more so than she had previously thought. In fact, after her off-campus semester, she shifted her career interest toward animal rights issues, and, the last I heard, she was serving as the executive director of a regional SPCA chapter.

Not every out of the classroom experience has to involve the kind of adventure and drama of an off-campus field semester like Southwest Field Studies. It would be a mistake to take from this that the more exotic and "strange" the experience, the bigger the educational outcome. Strange-land experiences can come in all shapes and sizes. From Mike Deibel's first foray onto Springwood Lake in a canoe to the American studies professor flipping the campus tour on its head, there are many possibilities to engage students with the unexpected and with uncertainty by leaving the classroom behind. Yet, taking on risky teaching like this *does* require a plan—even if you might need to adjust it on the fly several times along the way. There are general rules of thumb, design principles, and tricks of the trade that can help maximize the learning and the outcomes for you and for your students.

A PEDAGOGY FOR LEAVING THE CLASSROOM

Once you make the familiar, strange by taking your students out of the classroom, a whole host of design challenges come in to focus. When teaching in the classroom or lab, the structure and the routine play to our advantage in a variety of ways. You and your students know how to act and, at a basic level, what to do in class. For the most part, students sit in the same seats, you teach from the same place, and the activity that fills the time is controlled and controllable. But anyone who has attempted to do something as basic as take a class outside realizes that most of this flies out the window once you leave the building. Let's say on a nice, late spring day, you cave to demands and allow class to be held outside. First, there is the delay in getting there. Everyone has to pack up their stuff and shuffle out of the building. Then, you have to pick a suitable location— an area that is not too sunny, not too shady, level, with grass, but not muddy. Once you finally settle on the location, you have to manage the myriad distractions that inevitably crop up as you attempt to hold class. The noise from the lawn-mowing crew, a friend of one of your students calling out to them from across the quad, a bee that momentarily creates mass panic. It feels like a whole ton of work to manage it all—the time constraints, the location of learning, and the distractions.

In many ways, the challenges associated with moving class outside for the day are the same as those associated with more substantial forays out of the classroom. We have to manage transportation issues, the time constraints of the semester, the students' ability to stay focused and on task, and the location of learning. While teaching outside for the day is one thing, organizing a substantial community-based learning experience perhaps seems more daunting. But we can mitigate some of the teaching risks associated with leaving the classroom by adhering to several key design and facilitation principles along the way. And it should be noted that many of these principles apply just as readily to the work we do inside the classroom. Good pedagogy, it turns out, knows no boundaries.

FRAMING

Talk to any faculty member who has spent time teaching outside of the classroom in strange-land contexts and you will hear them talk about framing. Framing is the way we invite, introduce, and contextualize the learning activity that is about to take place. We frame learning all the time for students. A syllabus is, in essence, a frame. Talking about what you will be doing in the lab that day before students get started is a frame. You can frame an activity, a class, a unit, a semester, and even a four-year program. Good frames create meaning, prepare the students for learning, and build anticipation and engagement. We might call these, to borrow from Dewey, "educative" frames. Bad frames still create meaning, but the meaning they create is *miseducative*. As an example, think about how, even unintentionally, we could set up a community-based project that frames the activity as the neighborhood "needing our help," thus reinforcing negative, deficit-based stereotypes about local residents. This is still a frame for students, just a bad one. In addition to good frames and bad frames, there are also noneducative frames—frames that simply hold no meaning at all. Many times, we may think we have framed something well for students, only to realize later that they had absolutely no idea what the activity, unit, or exercise was about.

Framing out-of-classroom learning is critical because it will be unfamiliar to many students. As we take risks and experience the uncertainty, the mind scrambles to understand the new and novel context. If we don't work to create an educative frame for the learning, students will often react with confusion ("Why are we doing this?") or with negative preconceptions ("We have to do another stupid group project for my sociology class"). Good framing is an art form and takes some practice. I have learned over the years to avoid the twin sins of framing—overframing and underframing. Overframing occurs when we spend too much time explaining or contextualizing the learning in advance of students getting going and figuring it out. Once, on a tour with my family in Barcelona, Spain, we stood outside a cathedral with a tour guide for what seemed to be hours. She very patiently and thoroughly described everything about this wondrous cathedral—its history, its architecture, what we would find when we went inside, etc. My kids were mentally checked out after ten minutes. I hung on for another 20 until I, too, let my mind wander away from the square. By the time she released us to see the cathedral, we walked in with muted energy—the sense of discovery and newness was gone and, while the building was magnificent, there were few surprises. The tour guide had overframed the experience for us. Contrast this with another experience I had with students in New Zealand. On a day tour driving around Kaikoura—a region located on the east coast of the South Island—we stopped on the side of the road, and our guide announced with a sparkle in his eye, "There is something interesting just a few meters up the trail from here, why don't you go check it out?" We walked off the bus and into the forest curious and in an exploratory state. What we found I will never forget. After a short walk, we came upon a 30-foot waterfall cascading through the tree canopy and falling into a small, clear pool. Frolicking in the pool were at least 20 baby fur seals. It was a nursery where the adult fur seals kept their pups safe during the day when they were out in the ocean hunting for food. We spent time laughing and observing their behavior before walking back to the bus. Then, our guide did something important. He said, "What did you observe and what questions do you have?" We spent an hour outside the bus having a wonderful discussion about the life cycle of fur seals, the marine ecology of the Kaikoura peninsula, and New Zealand's ecotourism strategies, all emerging out of student observation and questions. This guide hadn't overframed the experience.

Under-framing occurs when you do the opposite. Students do not have enough to go on and struggle to make sense and meaning from the new and novel experience, environment, or context. Many times, while leading off-campus study, I would find myself annoyed when students wouldn't engage or appreciate some local expert or speaker that we had join the group for the day. Here was this amazing person sharing their life story or their wisdom, and our students would shuffle along seemingly bored without asking questions. This happened frequently enough, until I realized that the issue was that I had not properly framed for the students who this person was and why we had chosen to have them work with us for the day. To the students, it was just another day and a stranger. I began to more regularly and directly talk with students, in advance of guest speakers and lecturers, about the purpose of bringing in outside experts, about the importance of being curious and engaged learners in cross-cultural situations, and about the kinds of questions they might consider asking as it connected to our course content. I can't say it completely changed the dynamics for all time, but the engagement markedly improved. Uncertain and productively risky teaching and learning situations place students in novel and sometimes confusing contexts and states of being. Proper framing (not too much, not too little) helps orient the brain to the novelty and prepare the mind for what to look for and how to make sense of the experience.

LESS IS MORE

Connected to framing in out-of-classroom learning is the design principle of "less is more." Because we are asking students to learn in a more uncontrolled, unpredictable, and uncertain environment, we have to be much more judicious about content, activity, and assignment levels. To go back to our factory analogy, we can certainly be far more productive and efficient when we manage learning inside the four-walled classroom—not unlike a factory that makes a certain kind of widget. Because it is standardized and regularized, we can move through more widgets, more consistently, over time. But if, rather than lots of widgets, we wanted to produce *one great work of quality*, we would have to slow down and spend more time on the process. Out-of-classroom learning is like that. You will definitely do less with students in terms of volume of content. But what you lack in quantity, you can more than make up for in quality if you provide the time and space for students to engage.

There is another danger with less is more when it comes to out-of-classroom learning. I call it the "activity trap." Activity alone is not learning. Sometimes, in our zeal to plan, organize, and arrange for out-of-classroom experiences, we overdo it. When we let the itinerary dictate the curriculum, we have fallen into the activity trap. This is a particular vulnerability with short-term, study away experiences. Once, I served on a review committee for faculty who were planning off-campus May terms. We usually received around ten proposals to take students off campus to some location for three to four weeks in May as part of a course for academic credit. The proposals usually came from a mix of "old guard" faculty who had done these kinds of programs previously and "newbies" for whom this was their first foray into designing an off-campus study experience. As we looked at the various proposals each year, we would almost always return to the same theme in our feedback to newbie faculty members—they were planning to do way too much. One proposal to study sustainability and urban planning in Europe, for example, had the group visiting seven countries and cities in three and half weeks! The plan was for students to sleep on the train in between stops. We kindly suggested that this faculty member revise the itinerary with far fewer locations and deeper exploration of, say, three cities in total (and maybe a day off to, I don't know, do laundry?). And this is not just a concern about volume. Jamming too much travel, activity, or assignments into out-of-class learning environments is a set-up for failure. Inevitably in these contexts, things don't go according to plan. Your group misses a train, a guest speaker has to cancel, or half your students are out sick. There is always something. Just as we get enamored with content in the classroom, we can get seduced by the itinerary or the activity when doing out-of-class learning. By keeping our focus on doing less and using the time to examine issues in more depth, even if it seems risky that you are not doing enough, you give yourself and your students more room to manage the uncertainty and the unpredictable environment.

REFLECTION

A corollary to both of the preceding principles (framing and less is more) is the importance of reflection when it comes to out-of-class learning. Reflection is simply the conscious processing of experience. We reflect all the time in lots of different ways. But sometimes, and especially in learning situations, our reflection needs to be prompted and contextualized in order to get the most out of it. This is especially true when learning outside the classroom. One year, during my "Pedagogies of Place" class, I was reminded of the power of purposeful reflection. Each year I led this class, we would take a canoe trip down the Whitewater River on a Saturday to have an experiential sense of our local environment (and I used the river as an organizing theme of exploration in the class). While it was meant to be a fun day out, I also wanted students to experience and think about the historical, cultural, and ecological dynamics at play while on the river, and I wanted the experience to integrate with some of the readings we had for the week in a quiet and contemplative setting. This particular Saturday, I had failed to realize that I had organized our paddle on Labor Day weekend. When we arrived at the outfitter, the parking lot and landing were jam packed with holiday partyers and colorful local folk already halfway into a case of beer they were trailing alongside their various watercraft. There were canoes, tubes, rafts, kayaks, and inflatable flamingos. What I had envisioned when planning the syllabus was a meditative and meaningful paddle down a serene river, while exploring and experiencing the overall "sense of place." What we got, instead, was a four-hour immersion into local, southeast Indiana party culture. As we pulled the boats out at the end of the day, I worried about how class would go on the following Monday. What would we talk about? How can I make this experience meaningful? Should we just skip the class discussion about the trip and pivot to something else?

    I decided to stick with the original plan and walked into class on Monday with some trepidation and a plan B in the back pocket in case this went nowhere. I started by simply asking students what they thought of their experience on the river. The students had *a lot* to say. There were comments and jokes about the party behavior. Several students remarked on how disappointing it was that there were so many people on the river and that we didn't get any peace and quiet. But then, one student chimed in with an observation: "I wonder why we are criticizing these folks for their way of enjoying the river?" We all paused, and she went on. "I mean, isn't it kind of elitist to claim that our way of appreciating and experiencing place is better?" Another student picked up the thread: "That's true, it reminds me of how the environmental movement, in general, often dismisses working class and rural culture when it comes to what kinds of activities and conservation perspectives we value." Over the next 40 minutes, I barely got a word in—these students were off and running, reflecting on their experiences on the river and connecting them to class readings and course content in ways I had not even imagined. Never again would I question the value of reflection.

CONCLUSION

Clifford Geertz (1996) once wrote, "No one lives in the world in general." We live *in place*, and that place can often be ignored when it comes to teaching and learning in higher education. As David Gruenwald argued,

> The point of becoming more conscious of places in education is to extend our notions of pedagogy and accountability outward toward places. Thus extended, pedagogy becomes more relevant to the lived experience of students and teachers, and accountability is re-conceptualized so that places matter to educators, students, and citizens in tangible ways.
>
> (2003a, p. 646)

The risks involved in leaving the classroom can pale in comparison to the risks we take in turning our backs to our community—whether local, national, or international. The Association of American Colleges and Universities (AACU) report "A Crucible Moment," published in 2007, detailed the costs of such ignorance. The eye-opening report revealed that "the US ranked 139th in voter participation of 172 world democracies," while "just over one third of college faculty surveyed in 2007 strongly agreed that their campus actively promotes awareness of US or global social, political, and economic issues." In addition, the report stated, "35.8 percent of college students surveyed strongly agreed that faculty publicly advocate the need for students to become active and involved citizens," and "one third of college students surveyed strongly agreed that their college education resulted in increased civic capacities." Summarizing the findings, the report states,

> Moreover, the competencies basic to democracy cannot be learned only by studying books; democratic knowledge and capabilities are honed through hands-on, face-to-face, active engagement in the midst of differing perspectives about how to address common problems that affect the well-being of the nation and the world.
>
> (AACU, 2007)

Fourteen years after this report, the issues and challenges are only more pronounced. We are a nation and a world more polarized and more divided than we were in 2007. Increasingly, our college campuses struggle to have dialogue across differences and to sustain the kind of open and free exchange of ideas liberal democracy and liberal learning depend upon. Reconstructing democratic engagement can happen through classroom engagement. That is without question. Yet, classroom learning may be a necessary and insufficient context for the challenges of our times. Why do we take risks? Why do we engage with uncertainty? So that we may continue to learn, to grow, and to challenge ourselves, and, as a consequence, change our minds and, just maybe, change the world.

NOTE

1. The student's name has been changed.

REFERENCES

Association of American Colleges and Universities (AACU). *A crucible moment report.* (2007). Retrieved from: www.aacu.org/sites/default/files/files/crucible/highlights.pdf

Geertz, C., in Feld, S., & Basso, K. (Eds.). (1996). *Senses of place.* Santa Fe, NM: School for Advanced Research Press.

Gruenewald, D. A. (2003a). Foundations of place: A multidisciplinary framework for place-conscious education. *American Educational Research Journal, 40*(3), 619–654.

Gruenewald, D. A. (2003b). The best of both worlds: A critical pedagogy of place. *Educational Researcher, 32*(4), 3.

Kraft, R. J. (1992). Closed classrooms, high mountains and strange lands: An inquiry into culture and caring. In K. Warren, M. Sakofs, & J. Hunt (Eds.), *The theory and practice of experiential education* (pp. 8–15). Boulder, CO: Association for Experiential Education.

Sobania, N. (2015). *Putting the local in global education: Models for transformative learning through domestic off-campus programs.* Sterling, VA: Stylus Publishing.

Chapter 7
Assessing Uncertainty

INTRODUCTION

After teaching the same class for more than a few years, things can get pretty stale if you don't mix it up a bit. I had taught some version of my "Environment and Society" class for a while, and, as I sat in front of my computer during the summer before the scheduled fall class, I knew I wanted to try some new material—both in terms of content and also, importantly, in terms of class activities. Each year, I had a history unit where we did a quick survey through some of the key thinkers and historical figures in the US environmental movement. The class served as the introductory course to the major in environmental studies, and, like so many introductory and survey-oriented classes, the course was asked to do too much. In the past, I had ripped through three weeks of lectures and fairly dry historical material in an attempt to give students some grounding in the historical figures and movements in the United States. If they wanted more, they could follow up by taking one of our upper-level electives in environmental history. But as a department, we agreed that all students should get *some* environmental history as part of the major. That is how I wound up with a three-week unit on environmental history that was not doing anyone any favors. For my students, it was pretty dry because I had to lecture more than I might like to get through the volume of content. For me, it felt rushed. I felt as though we were just skimming the surface, and, as a result, students didn't seem to be retaining much of the material when it came time for the unit quiz. And, perhaps more importantly from my point of view, they just didn't seem as engaged as I would have liked.

So there I sat in my office, listening to the soothing hum of the air-conditioning unit on a way too humid August morning and staring at the blinking cursor on my computer screen wondering what to do about this unit. Then, I had an idea. My daughter had just experienced a murder mystery birthday party and had come home raving about how much fun it was. "What if I designed the unit like a murder mystery?" I thought. I sometimes have strange, out of the blue thoughts like this, and I have learned, over time, to do my best to quiet the little voice in my head that tells me why something won't work and just let the thoughts run for a bit before pulling back on the leash. So, I kept thinking. "I could assign each student a historical character, one of the key figures from US environmental history, and have them do research." Ok, sounds simple enough, but where does the murder come in? "What if, alongside the historical research, I added a murder mystery plot involving all the characters?" Sure, but how would you have them enact the mystery? Over the three-week period in each class? "That would take too long. How about during one full class? We could host a tea party in class and they could come dressed in their period-appropriate clothes." My mind went on like this for a while. I would raise a challenge or concern in my head, but, after thinking more on it, I could usually find a way around whatever was concerning me. But then I hit a real snag: "How am I going to assess this?"

ASSESSING ASSESSMENT

Assessment is one of those areas of higher education that gets a bad rap. And perhaps deservedly so. The bureaucratization of education has no better poster child than the tangled web of curriculum maps, outcomes models, learning objective rubrics, and accreditation reports that now seem to dominate the attention of deans, department chairs, and chief academic officers. It is easy to criticize this as "busywork" that distracts from our central mission of teaching and learning. I recall one time, when I was serving as a member of the assessment committee at my former institution, I went to speak with the natural science division about the necessity of creating an assessment map of learning outcomes in courses and majors. This was a cruel assignment. As a relatively young assistant professor, I was given the short end of the stick and entered into that division meeting knowing I had my work cut out for me. I did my best—describing why assessment was central to institutional improvement and how our accreditors were asking for this information. But the faculty were not buying what I was selling. After patiently listening to my lame pitch, an older faculty member finally spoke up. "Jay, we already do assessment, it's called grading." I tucked my tail in and slinked out of that meeting, realizing this assessment thing was a lot harder than it looked.

But there are other ways to view assessment. I often like to reframe assessment as a question: "How do we know that what we are doing is working?" Posed in this way, a course grade doesn't tell us a whole lot. On the other hand, course grades *can* tell us a lot if we look at them in aggregate. We are learning, for example, that an examination of DFW rates (D and F grades plus withdrawals) in introductory science courses can reveal disturbing trends. Historically underrepresented students (first generation and students of color) can, for example, have much higher DFW rates than the rest of the student population. A recognition of this inequity has led to a call for more active learning, more iterative feedback, and more structure in introductory STEM courses to set students up for success (Report to the President,

2012). In courses that implement these measures, DFW rates can drop significantly (Freeman et al., 2014; Haake, HilleRisLambers, Pitre, Freeman, 2011). Chalk one up in the win column for assessment!

Yet, as I was staring at my computer screen with visions of creative, active learning designs floating in my head, I was still struggling with how to assign grades for this unit. I had envisioned an in-class tea party where students would show up in period-appropriate costumes and act out their parts. But what was I going to do? Grade their clothing choices? Or their theatrical prowess? The more I thought about it, the more I wanted to retreat to safer harbors. "Maybe I should just assign a paper," I thought. "Or, we could just do a unit quiz at the end." The need to produce a grade for students—both on individual assignments and for the course as a whole—is a given and tends to drive our whole process of course and unit design. But, the funny thing is, we rarely stop and think about this thing we call a "grade." As academics, we encourage our students to think critically and challenge the given, and yet, here we sit, organizing entire courses and tracks of study around a thing that few of us have ever critically considered. Where did grades come from? Why is the system organized in this way (A, B, C, D, and F)? And, whatever happened to "E"?!

MAKING THE GRADE

Cathy Davidson, in her book *The New Education*, discusses the history of grades in the United States and writes,

> the apparatus of grading and judging, assessing and failing students—including bell curves, grades, and standardized testing—were fully developed in the nineteenth century. . . . The methods we still use for evaluating student achievement were adopted from quantifiable measures of productivity developed for factories and the brand new assembly lines.

(2017, pp. 200–201)

As with the architecture and systems of schooling we take for granted today—the bells, individual classroom periods, and divisions by age—grades and standardized assessments are a vestige of the modern industrial age. Before this period, assessment of student progress was largely narrative and qualitative. Grades share a similar history. According to Davidson,

> [t]he term "grade" seems to have come from the idea that students wouldn't "make the grade" in the same way that an imperfectly manufactured product would "fail to make the grade" by falling off a sloped conveyer belt in an assembly process.

(Ibid., p. 203)

The Mount Holyoke College faculty were the first to adopt a letter grade system in 1897 (Davidson, 2017). And this is where the story gets downright bizarre. The faculty seemed to have no issue with moving from a narrative, handwritten feedback system to numerical grades. That wasn't the major point of contention. What was far more controversial was the grading system itself. Originally, the system was to be organized in descending order, as in A, B, C, D, E, with E being the failing grade. However, some faculty apparently thought an E as the failing grade would be confusing as students might think E stood for "effort" or "excellent." So, according to Davidson, "Mount Holyoke adopted the F, justified by the Anglo-Norman *failer*, meaning nullification, nonoccurrence, or failure" (Ibid., p. 204). The new system would be A, B, C, D, F (skipping that pesky controversial and confusing E), and it was soon adopted by other colleges. Yet, in another strange twist, this system was then introduced to the American meat-packing industry by an Illinois professor of agriculture. While the meat-packing industry found much to like about the system, they believed it to be too reductive in explaining the complexities of their product, so they insisted on adding written comments alongside their "grade A" steak. Apparently, the assessment of red meat requires more nuance than the system we continue to faithfully and uncritically implement in our schools.

FEAR OF FAILURE

This leads to another taken-for-granted vestige of our current assessment system: failure. The F as a failing grade carries with it a host of assumptions about learning and the educational process. Educational anthropologist Ray McDermott once wrote, "Failure is waiting, every morning and in every classroom in the United States. Before children or their teachers arrive, failure is there. Somebody is going to fail. It is a cultural rule" (McDermott, 1997, p. 130). While this is now changing rapidly, for many years, higher education was organized around the assumption that some students would (and perhaps even should) flunk out. Faculty would begin courses suggesting that a certain percentage of the students wouldn't pass—either as some sort of motivational tool or to weed out troublemakers. There were stories of new student week convocation addresses where some senior administrator would tell students to look to their right and to their left, because "one of your classmates won't make it through to the sophomore year." Gateway courses were structured in majors to weed out "weaker" students and reduce numbers before they could enter into upper-level coursework. All this led to a system that accepted failure as a given and necessary part of the educational process. Dropouts and retention were not a concern and, in some contexts, were even seen as a point of pride. However, as Bridgette Burns, executive director of the University Innovation Alliance and one of the leading thinkers on student success, declared in the opening keynote address to the 2018 UIA National Summit: "The higher education system . . . was actually perfectly set-up and designed to fail students."

As higher education has changed and expanded to include more students and a greater diversity of learners, this approach to failure has begun to shift. College is no longer the domain of the chosen few. And, in a sense, the democratization of access to higher education has almost been too successful. It is now a standard assumption that a bachelor's degree is a necessary ticket into the middle class, even as that assumption is increasingly being questioned. And, as state funding has dropped along with the precipitous rise in college expenses and the gutting of the middle class in the United States, colleges and universities can no longer afford a "50% scrap rate." While the old way of thinking was that such a state of affairs was indicative of rigor, the new way of thinking is all about student success. Or, perhaps more crassly, revenue. It is far less expensive to work to retain the student you have already attracted and enrolled than it is to go find a new student. Institutions have realized this and are now working on developing retention measures—a near 180-degree reversal of the old paradigm of failure. Now, rather than intimidating students about academic rigor during new student orientation, we have "welcome week" focused on inclusion, belonging, and support. Instead of gateway courses in majors, we are redesigning introductory classes to maximize student success through inclusive pedagogy and universal design for learning. And, instead of touting dropout rates, institutions are now laser focused on completion rates. Failure, it turns out, is no longer an option.

Yet, while we aim to eliminate the "big F" failures that we attribute to grading and dropping out, in risky teaching we actually want to create *more* opportunities for students to experience "small f" failures in learning. Manu Kapor coined the term "productive failure," which he defined as "engaging students in solving complex, ill-structured problems without the provision of support structures" (2008, p. 379). In essence, Kapor designed learning environments for science students where the activities and exercises were purposefully set up for students to fail due to the ill-structured nature of the problems. Kapor explains,

> learners may explore, struggle, and even fail at solving ill-structured problems. The process may well be less efficient in the shorter term but it may also allow for learning that is potentially more flexible and adaptive in the longer term. Persisting with such a process may engender increasingly high levels of complexity in the exploration of the problem and solution spaces. In turn, this build-up of complexity may allow for learning that is potentially more flexible and adaptive. . . . [This] give[s] us reason to believe that there may well be a hidden efficacy in students solving ill-structured problems without any support or scaffolds even if it seems to lead to failure in the shorter term.
>
> (Ibid., p. 382)

The qualities that we want for all our students, such as persistence, grit, and self-efficacy, paradoxically may come not from avoiding failure but from failing more. The key difference, however, in "little f" failure is the low-stakes nature of the failures. Students fail fast and fail forward in this approach.

Yet, as faculty, we still must grade student assignments, proctor exams, and submit grades. How can one try risky teaching and approaches such as productive failure while still adhering to our rigid system of assessment? This is a question I am asked almost every time I give talks and workshops with faculty. "I would love to try some of these things," a faculty member might say, "but I have no idea how I would give grades on it." What Holly Clark (2015) described as the "culture of one right answer" still dominates how we think about assessment. Multiple choice exams, "high-stakes" tests, and other traditional forms of assessment allow for a more straightforward system of grading. A student submits their work, the instructor grades it by checking to see if the student got answers "right" or "wrong," and, in the end, we wind up with some sort of numeric or quantitative score—85% or a B. In courses and disciplines where the student assessment is more narrative based, there has always been an allowance for more creativity and flexibility in grading. The fine arts and some humanities and social science disciplines have used rubrics, reflective essays, portfolios, presentations, and the like to expand beyond the more traditional multiple choice and short answer tests. Some faculty have even decided to take the riskiest move of all and reject grading entirely. Jesse Stommel (2018) noted, in a blog post titled "How to Ungrade" that,

> The work of grading is framed less in terms of giving feedback or encouraging learning and more as a way of ranking students against one another. Nods to "fairness" are too often made for the sake of defensibility rather than equity. What disturbs me is how effortlessly and casually this language rolls off Education's collective tongue. And I'm even more disturbed by how many otherwise productive pedagogical conversations get sidetracked by the too easily internalized ubiquity of grades.

"Ungrading" as a term was even recently featured in the *Chronicle of Higher Education* (Supiano, 2019) as a protest movement of sorts against our current assessment system.

DESIGNING FOR RISKY ASSESSMENT

If we are going to try riskier forms of teaching and learning, we have to expand our mental models of assessment to go along with it. Assessment, even with the best efforts of the ungrading movement, is not going away anytime soon. What we can do is attempt to align our assessment and grading strategies with the new forms of teaching and learning that are emerging. And, it turns out, many of these tools and principles are more effective for students and more, yes, fun for you as a teacher. I often encourage faculty to think about grading and assessment the way we think about birthday parties. At your birthday party, you sit there with a whole pile of wrapped presents in front of you. These gifts are from people you know well and who know you. They have thought about and selected your present with intention and purpose and carefully wrapped it for you to open and enjoy. As the recipient of this splendor, you look at this pile of goodness with excitement and anticipation. Not the way you view grading? When I find myself bored to tears while grading, I try not to blame the students, I blame the assignment. Usually, my frustration at reading student responses means I have structured an assessment poorly or I have asked a boring question.

For example, I often work with faculty who are frustrated with the quality of the student reflections in journal assignments. They typically complain that students do the minimum required and tend to write vacuous reflections that simply regurgitate what they experienced with minimal to no critical analysis or integration with course content. These types of reflection assignments can be hideous to read and grade. I know, I've been there. But, there is a rule of thumb I once learned from my information technology (IT) colleagues. We were in a meeting about something called "data governance" (a new phrase for me), which basically entailed making sure that the college had a way to organize and manage its various forms and streams of data. As it turned out, we were not managing it very well at all, and it was causing problems when it came time to turn that data into actionable knowledge. One of my IT colleagues finally said the obvious, "Garbage in, garbage out." If we don't make sure the data have integrity when we put them *in*, they won't be any use to us when we take them *out* and analyze them. A similar thing could be said about reflection assignments. If you ask a crappy question or construct a sloppy writing prompt, you will pay for it on the backend with a whole pile of boring, vacuous reflections to grade. Garbage in, garbage out. If we can avoid assigning garbage, we won't have to collect it. There *are* times when I feel like that birthday boy when grading and I can't wait to see what my students have done. That is when I know I have structured an assignment right. The challenge is to learn how to make high-quality assessments by design rather than by accident. More often than not, I have found that taking risks in assessment, like taking risks in teaching, can bring about positive results—both for me and for my students.

This is true in more quantitative, STEM fields as well. I recall a former colleague of mine, a biologist, who designed this wonderfully creative assignment in her upper-level molecular biology course. She noticed that *Wikipedia* was missing information and up-to-date research about a certain kind of protein that she and the class had been studying. So, she constructed an assignment that was, in essence, learn enough about this protein over the course of the semester to be able to edit and improve the *Wikipedia* entry. This had all the hallmarks of an effective, risky assessment. The assignment was relevant, connected to something that mattered in the world, and effectively integrated into course content and learning goals. It required students to demonstrate their new knowledge in a novel context. And, they were demonstrating that new knowledge to an authentic audience—in this case, the *entire world*. Anyone who has ever tried to edit pages on *Wikipedia* knows that there are people out there who watch and review such edits carefully. And, if they are inaccurate or just plain no good, they are flagged or edited out. The students knew their entry had to be good enough to pass the test of a watchful scientific community. The professor could have just assigned a standard research paper or given a final, high-stakes test. But instead, she tried something riskier. As a result, the student work that semester took on a much different tone and sense of responsibility, and, at the end of the semester, I can guarantee she couldn't wait to see what they had done.

Going beyond the traditional multiple choice tests, final exams, written papers, and high-stakes assignments can be risky. Students are as much creatures of habit as we are, and most of them have spent a lifetime in school, especially in the post– No Child Left Behind era in the United States, where standardized testing is the norm. A K–12 teacher friend of mine referred to this as the Texas educational model: "Sit, git, spit, and forgit." There are some basic design principles that have helped me move off of the well-worn tracks of grading and assessment and into riskier, uncertain terrain. When I think about courses, activities, and assignments now, I use these principles to help me think through how I can best align my risky teaching with risky assessment.

ITERATION AND THE ART OF FAILING FORWARD

One way to think about risky assessment is to emphasize looking forward rather than backward. If we are not careful, assessment can become a kind of manic pack-rat activity of collection and storage. We ask for "learning artifacts" and collect portfolios. We crunch numbers and revel in spreadsheets. We produce reports and narratives. And it all goes on a shelf somewhere for posterity. Or, I suppose in the modern day, it gets stored on a shared drive. We can become intoxicated by data. But the point of data collection, and assessment, is to turn that into actionable improvement. We can think of assessment as a process along a continuum: data→information→knowledge→wisdom. In this continuum, information is a meaningful collection of data. Knowledge is a meaningful collection of information. And, at the end, wisdom is generated from a meaningful collection of knowledge. The problem in education is that we tend to spend too much time on the left side of this continuum (data and information) and not enough time on the right side (knowledge and wisdom). Accreditors have learned this over time, and now they insist that institutions demonstrate not just what they have collected in terms of data but how they have closed the loop by turning assessment data and information into institutional knowledge and wisdom.

At the classroom level, looking forward rather than just backward with assessment is the difference between formative and summative assessment. Summative assessment is the assessment *of* learning. We do lots of summative assessment in higher education. I remember, as a college student in the 1990s, writing in the dreaded "blue books." These blue, stapled, and lined paper books were nearly universally used for in-class writing exams. We students would show up, pick up the exam, sit down at a desk, and write nonstop for 2–3 hours. At the end, my hand was cramped up into a gnarled ball and the last several pages were barely legible. We would dutifully turn in those blue books and then never see or think about them again. Some weeks later, our letter grade for the course would show up in the mail. Summative assessment. The problem with summative assessment is that it is backward looking. Looking at your grade on a paper you just wrote tells you how you "performed" writing that paper. But, it doesn't necessarily help you with your *next* paper. Good writing instructors know this. They know that to actually *improve* students' writing, rather than just *judge* students' writing, you have to give them lots of opportunities to practice and receive feedback in a low-stakes environment. This is where formative assessment comes in.

Formative assessment is assessment *for* learning. It is forward looking and tends to be iterative. In higher education, we have not historically done a lot of formative assessment. However, that is changing as we learn more about the best and most effective kinds of teaching and learning environments. Several years ago, I was chatting with a colleague of mine over the winter exam period as he was lamenting the huge stack of papers he had to grade. As we talked, he recounted his grading and assignment approach. He asked his students to write a 20- to 30-page paper as the final assignment for the course, and it counted for 50 percent of the total grade. He would then dutifully read all 30 exams and make comments in the margins as well as in a long summative commentary at the end of the paper, followed by the grade. I asked him if I could see an example. As I looked through the sample student paper, I noticed that he was marking up *a lot*: Grammar and spelling mistakes, poor sentence construction, bad paragraph transitions along with claims without evidence, ineffectively framed thesis statements, etc. And at the end of the paper comments were quite, shall we say, "judgy." They were mostly about what the student missed, did poorly, or failed to adequately explain. Then, there was the circled letter at the bottom: "C+."

The thing with assessment like this is that it can be ineffective in two specific ways. First, from the student perspective, this kind of summative evaluation does not promote improvement. Students tend to receive the paper and quickly flip to the last page to look at the grade. After a brief smile or frown, the whole endeavor is forgotten. It is a rare student who reads the summative comments at the end, much less the comments and corrections in the margins. So, really, why are we as teachers spending time on that? And this gets us to the other way this time-honored form of grading is ineffective. It is ineffective for the faculty member from the standpoint of time management. We wind up spending a lot of time grading papers like this when what we are really doing is talking to ourselves.

With my colleague, I suggested a different approach. I told him that if he was concerned about grammar issues, he could mark up one paragraph as an example and ask the student to note where the general issues were and work on improving them (perhaps with the help of the writing center). Then, I suggested he only note three things in the summative comments at the end of the paper: The three most important things for this student to know to help her improve her paper. Finally, I suggested perhaps the riskiest thing of all—give her the chance to rewrite the paper incorporating the suggested improvements for extra credit. If she elected to do so, ask her to include a cover page that describes how and where she responded to the suggested improvements. This allows the teacher to quickly identify where to focus and means you don't have to reread (and grade) the whole paper from scratch. If this sounds like the way we go through the "revise and resubmit" peer review process as scholars, it is. If we do this for our peers to help improve their work, why don't we do it for our students? A semester later, my colleague sent me an email thanking me for the suggestions. He now assigned smaller assignments and provided shorter, just-in-time feedback more regularly. He also no longer had to endure his usual postsemester grading marathon gauntlet. Doing formative assessment this way does take planning. You need to schedule in time for the iterative process and allow for feedback. But, it can actually take *less* overall time. You wind up giving *more* feedback, of a shorter kind, more frequently. This is assessment worth doing because it is focused on student success and learning. So, when designing assignments and a general assessment approach to your class, think about the principle of iteration. How can students fail fast and fail forward? How can you give multiple opportunities for practice, feedback, and revision? How can you incentivize growth and improvement rather than a culture of one right answer?

CHOICE AND TAKING OWNERSHIP OF LEARNING

Another form of and approach to risky assessment is to prioritize and offer more opportunities for student choice. Choice is an important part of students feeling a sense of ownership over their learning. Generally speaking, we don't like being told what to do, and this is certainly the case for students in higher education. But importantly, that does not mean letting students do whatever they want. Somewhere in between these extremes of absolute freedom and absolute constraint is the space we want to play in with our students—a space I call "bounded choice." As faculty, we help set the frame, what Ronald Heifetz calls the "holding space," for the work to be done. To Heifetz, a "holding environment consists of any relationship in which one party has the power to hold the attention of another party and facilitate adaptive work" (Heifetz, 2009, p. 105). As faculty, we have power and authority in the classroom that we cannot cede even if we wanted to. We have the power to hold attention as Heifetz argues. But within that frame or space, there is also the opportunity for choice and, crucially, student ownership over their learning.

For example, with my murder mystery assignment, I didn't want to simply pick historical characters for my students. Instead, I gave them a brief questionnaire that asked them to detail some of their interests and preferences when it came to learning more about environmental history. Were they drawn to recent history or perhaps something from the 19th or 18th century? Did the gender or the racial identity of the person matter to them? Were they more interested in natural history and biology? Social and environmental justice? From this questionnaire, I attempted to match a key figure to the student. In my matchmaking communication back to each student, I explained why I had selected the person I did for them. While they didn't have total choice over the process, I attempted to honor their preferences and interests. Students expressed an appreciation for the care and thought that went into the process and, I think, bought in to the assignment more as a result.

Another time in a different class, I tried something with student choice that felt quite risky. We were getting toward the end of the semester, and it was time to start thinking about the dreaded final exam. I had grown tired of the usual ways of constructing a final exam and wanted to try something different. About two weeks before the final, I told the students that we were going to have a series of review classes in preparation for exam week. Nothing particularly innovative about that. But, I told them to be sure to bring all their course materials to class—notebooks, handouts, texts, etc. During class, I broke them out into groups and had each subgroup tackle the material from about one quarter of the semester and syllabus. Their task was to review back through the material and come up with an "exam" for that section. The exam could be short answer questions, essay questions, or any combination they could consider. Then I informed them that if the questions were good enough, they would become the final exam. It was, I told them, a do-it-yourself final. It was amazing to watch them work that week. With the knowledge that they had the ability and the choice to make their own exam, they were free to explore and create. They reviewed the course material with much more engagement and interest than my typical review sessions, and they discussed, in animated fashion, what would be on "their exam." After each group finished its part, we came together as a class to discuss and finalize the questions for the final. There were no "gotcha" questions and a whole lot less stress about the exam itself. The students chose questions and topics to address what really interested them and what they wanted to explore. They had to compromise among themselves about what comprised a "good question" and to ensure proper comprehensive coverage for the content of the semester. And they worked *hard* to make that exam. At one point, a student sat back and remarked, "Aw man, now we have to actually *take* this!" The questions were good. And they were *hard*. Adding student choice into assessment, when done well, isn't a cop-out or a way to let students off the hook. Done well, it can be *more* rigorous and demanding of students.

There are lots of ways to involve student choice and a sense of ownership in assessment. I have seen faculty, at the beginning of an assigned paper, build the grading rubric for the assignment *with* the students as part of a class discussion. Students often know what goes into a good paper, and by asking and involving them in the construction of the grading rubric, you accomplish several things. First, students feel a sense of ownership over the assignment and how they will be assessed. Second, it serves as a way to set a group norm and expectation for what makes for a good paper. Third, it mitigates the "grade grubbing" that can come after the assignment and assessment where students argue with you about "fairness" or complain about unclear expectations. Because the rubric was built together as a class, those issues tend to be addressed on the front end. Finally, it fosters metacognition and overt thinking about the learning process itself. A class discussion about "what makes a good paper" is transferable to other classes and assignments—even if the key takeaway is that there are *multiple* forms and archetypes of good papers.

Another way you can increase choice is to have students select the kind of assessment they prefer—either individually or collectively. Final assignments, for example, could be in the form of a traditional written paper, a vlog (video blog), a digital story, or perhaps a one-on-one reflection session with the instructor. While creating this kind of multimodal variability does take work on the front end for you as the instructor, in my experience, it pays dividends on the back end with increased student engagement and effort in completing an assignment that they chose. The key, as with all forms of risky assessment, is to clarify expectations and outcomes for the assignment. Providing archetypes and examples of excellent work can be helpful for students if it is the first time they have experienced this type of assignment. Rubrics can also help, though it is important to keep them simple, straightforward, and connected directly to course learning goals. Ensuring that you have a few check-in points along the way can also keep students on track and limit last minute "cramming," which in nontraditional forms of assessment often leads to poor final products. These can be a combination of peer reviews, "drafty drafts" that you assess, or even in-class presentations on progress. Nothing lights a fire under students more than opportunities for peer (and public) feedback. In the end, with increased effort, you tend to get a better final product—something that is both an effective demonstration of learning and more enjoyable to grade.

Finally, one other approach to increase student choice and ownership is to metaphorically "give them the keys to the car." For example, ask students to grade themselves—they are often a *much* harsher critic than you would be. Involve them in constructing assessments and assignments in various ways. Can they design unit quizzes? Perhaps in teams? You can even, if you want to go all in on choice, ask students to build the syllabus with you at the beginning of the semester. One year, I purposefully left a six-week chunk of my syllabus, toward the middle of the semester, completely blank. As we discussed the course in that first class meeting, the students looked at me quizzically when it came time to talk about the blank space in the syllabus. "What we do with that time is up to us," I said. "Do you mean, we could do *anything*?!" one student asked incredulously. "Within reason and based on the learning goals for the course, yes," I replied. Another student chimed in: "Can we build a boat?" "That depends on why you think it would be important to do as it relates to what we are trying to accomplish in this class," I replied. More ideas and comments spun around the room as the students imagined what might be possible in that curious, blank-looking section of the syllabus. A few days later, a colleague caught me in the hall. "I hear you are building a boat in your class this semester." Student choice does have its risks.

AUTHENTICITY AND AUDIENCE

Another way to consider productively riskier forms of assessment is to make assignments more "authentic." By authentic, I mean asking students to demonstrate their learning in some form or fashion that matters—to them and ideally to others. Make the assignment matter to someone *other* than just the teacher and the student. So much of assessment and grading are private acts. Students toil by themselves on a paper only to submit it to a faculty member for grading. Quizzes and exams are most often taken and graded individually. Rarely do peers get a chance to see each other's work. Even rarer still is a student's work seen outside of a given class or department. Most rare of all is for a student's work to matter to the world beyond the campus boundaries. This is perhaps slightly less true in the arts, where there is a long tradition of the "critique" and the studio where students have a chance to see each other's work and offer feedback. Music and theater students perform their learning quite publicly in front of audiences—often including the general public. Creative writing pedagogy has a long history of peer review and discussion of work. In these fields and worlds, there has always been a public dimension to how a student demonstrates learning. However, in many disciplines, there is rarely, if ever, a public dimension. A STEM student may study for an exam with others, but when it comes time to take the test, it is on her own. A history major writes a 20-page research paper that only the professor sees. Using the principle of authenticity and audience in assessment invites new and riskier forms of assignments and grading that have the potential to increase student engagement and success.

One example of this in practice is the work of Gabriella Weaver, professor of chemistry, at the University of Massachusetts Amherst. Dr. Weaver, along with several of her colleagues interested in chemical education at other institutions, were noticing the high DFW rates in their courses and the attrition rate between the first and second years. As they dug into the data, it was also alarmingly clear that the melt was coming disproportionately from underrepresented groups. Those early discussions led to funding from the National Science Foundation and the creation of the Center for Authentic Science Practice in Education (CASPiE). The focus of the center was to redesign undergraduate laboratory courses to bring real research into the curriculum thus making the laboratory research experience more like the authentic practice of science. The traditional model was for students to get into a research lab to engage in real research much later in their career—usually their junior or senior year. But, given the melt Dr. Weaver and her colleagues were noticing, this was too late. Dr. Weaver recalled realizing,

> there's a whole population of students that we are losing and there is an opportunity, if we redesign undergraduate research, to bring those students in. So, we developed these modules for students to do real research in the undergraduate labs for first and second year Chemistry students.
>
> (2019, personal communication)

The model involves students completing research in collaborative groups with access to advanced instrumentation as part of the mainstream science curriculum. The idea was to enable students to experience an authentic research environment—one that included a fair amount of uncertainty for both the students and the instructor. Dr. Weaver noted,

> you can't just throw students into the deep end and say, "here is what to solve, go." There is this art to it. Knowing how much to give them, where to put the boundaries, how much scaffolding they need, and how much you let them explore. And by letting them explore, as a faculty member, you have to move out of your own comfort zone . . . letting them do what some people call failure. It's not failure. This is exactly what we do in science.

The CASPiE model was one of the early precursors to what is now widely known as CURE—course-based undergraduate research experience—where students complete original research in their laboratory courses alongside supervising faculty instructors. These forms of authentic assignments and assessments have been shown to increase persistence, self-efficacy, and critical thinking in science education (Chase et al., 2017).

INTEGRATION AND THE WHOLE STUDENT

In addition to increasing student choice and authenticity in our assignments and assessments, risky teaching invites us to extend our perspective beyond the cognitive domain and the content of the course itself. Traditionally, our charge as faculty (and what our accreditors expect) is that we organize our syllabi and assignments based upon the academic content of the course and in a way that is connected to the larger frameworks of the discipline and the major. This makes sense for obvious reasons. But, the larger educational goals of the institution as whole, or the four-year trajectory of learning that a student may experience, rarely fit neatly into discrete courses or even the major. Ask a student what he or she remembers most about a particular class and you will rarely hear discrete content. Instead, you will hear metalearning of various shapes and sizes. Some of it is most certainly intellectual, cognitive, or "academic" in nature: "I didn't know and was amazed to learn that public schools are more segregated now than they were before *Brown v. Board of Education*." Or: "I learned how to write more clear and effective thesis statements." Often, though, the key and significant learning is integrational in nature.

> At first, I hated that class. I was confused and overwhelmed. But then, I decided to ask for help from the faculty member, which was scary, but after that, I was much more comfortable and did much better. It made me realize asking for help is a key part of being a successful student.

These integrated learning outcomes are often the most powerful and long lasting for a student. They often appear when departments, schools, or institutions construct so-called general education learning outcomes. As an aside, I wonder why we continue to insist on calling these goals general education? Often, they represent our highest educational aspirations as an institution of higher learning. These goals are what, at the end of the day, we hope our students become as they move out into the world. If well-articulated and mission-driven, these goals and objectives can be powerful characteristics of a life well-lived. And yet, given all of that, we call them general education goals, and we advise students to take them early in their careers to "get them out of the way." And is it any wonder when our students ask us, "Why do I have to take this?" Would it be that much of a risk to make these aspirational and integrative goals more central and overt to a student's four-year experience?

Whether on the classroom or institutional scale, productively risky assessment often involves forms of integrated learning. The Association of American Colleges and Universities (AACU) definition of integrated learning is "an understanding and a disposition that a student builds across the curriculum and co-curriculum, from making simple connections among ideas and experiences to synthesizing and transferring learning to new, complex situations within and beyond the campus" (AACU, 2009). Students can integrate across courses within a major, they can integrate across courses outside of their field or division, they can integrate between the curriculum and co-curriculum, and they can integrate between their college experiences and their life in general. And, by the way, they are doing this all the time with or without our help. Our colleagues in student development offices know this well. They are the ones who see and interact with students outside the classroom and have the opportunity to hear and watch how students are making sense of their total college experience. As faculty, we are sometimes limited in our view of students—they come into our classroom world for a short window of time, and we often don't ask or have the opportunity to know what else goes on in a student's life. Some faculty prefer this and I don't want to suggest here that we should have no boundaries between our lives and our students' lives. That said, risky teaching is relational, and students want to know that we care about them not as "brains on a stick" but as whole persons with a range of emotions and life experiences. The recent events (whether the global pandemic or the racial reckoning in the United States) quickly reveal that, for many students and for our students of color in particular, it is impossible *not* to integrate their lived experiences into their academic learning. In a very real sense, the personal is pedagogical.

One simple way to encourage more integrated learning in courses is to design assessments that ask for it. One year, I designed a "flex class" into my syllabus that we wound up not needing (that was a first). It was on the last week of the semester, and I had been running around all week without a second to think about a class plan for the day. At the last minute, I came up with an idea. I walked into class and declared, "Today we will be doing a pop quiz! Please take out a piece of paper." Groans and eye rolls all around. I told them it would be a different sort of pop quiz, something I was calling the "unfinal." The eye rolling stopped and the students shared curious looks. I asked them to take ten minutes of free writing to answer the following prompt: "In what ways did this course's content, readings, and/or activities integrate with other aspects of your life at Earlham?" I told them they might think about other courses they have taken, something they experienced outside of class, life experiences they have had, etc. I had no idea how this would go and half expected they would be done quickly and not even take up the full ten minutes. To my surprise, by the end of the allotted time, most were still immersed in writing. Once they were done, I asked them to share with a neighbor and then summarize key integrations with the class as a whole. What I heard astounded me. They shared about a range of classes from across the curriculum—many I never even considered to be connected to what we had done in this class. They shared about experiences they had on the athletic fields, in internships and work study, and in the dorms. The hour flew by and I knew I had a winner. Since then, my flex day has stayed on every syllabus for every course I have taught, and the unfinal is a mainstay risky assessment activity.

CONCLUSION

The day had finally arrived for the assigned murder mystery tea party in my Environment and Society class. I came to work that morning a little anxious about how this would all go. I had reserved a special room designed for hosting guests at the college, which had a fireplace and more formal furniture, just to provide a bit more ambiance. And I used department funding to have the whole affair catered with tea and cookies to sweeten the deal. Still, I was not entirely sure what I was going to get, other than a group of grumpy, sleepy college students wearing wigs. As the students began to file in, a big smile came across my face. They were totally into this. "Aristotle" showed up barefoot in a toga. "Thoreau" was in a top hat. "Rachel Carson" was wearing a wig and a rather sensible fishing vest. Once they had all arrived, had their tea, and mingled a bit, I asked them to silently form a history line—from oldest guest to youngest. It took a few tries but they finally got it. Then, more mingling as they learned about each other's lives, key accomplishments in environmental thinking, and who they liked and didn't like in the group. I had written fake murder mystery character backstories for each one. It turned out that John Muir and Edward Abbey *really* didn't like Gifford Pinchot, and, at the scheduled time, poor Gifford cried out and collapsed to the floor, dead. Accusations flew about: "It was Rachel Carson! She told me that she and Gifford had a lover's quarrel last night," said one student. "No, it was Aldo Leopold," said another. "He is still mad about a piece of land Gifford ruined for timber." After much animated discussion, it was determined that it was, in fact, Edward Abbey who murdered Pinchot—all because he just didn't like his utilitarian ideals.

The students left "class" that day in a buzz. I was walking on air, myself. It was a wildly successful class, and there were more than a few curious onlookers in the building as my students, some in full drag, sauntered out for their next class. I felt a sense of satisfaction that my risky teaching brainstorm from the summer had panned out about as well as I could have hoped. But I learned much more in taking this risk as an instructor than just a fun active learning exercise to teach environmental history. Back in the summer when I was in brainstorming mode, I worked hard to think through how I would assess this unit. I didn't just want to give an exam at the end, nor did I want to make things too easy for the students and just give them all A's for costume design and performance. I ended up doing several things. First, each student was required to complete a paper on their assigned character—outlining the person's biography and their contributions to environmental thinking. I assigned a peer review iterative assessment step where students would get feedback on an early draft based on a rubric we developed as a class. I also developed a rubric for the tea party itself—giving students extra points for their engagement with their character and the event (Aristotle scored big here—it was a cold day in November). Finally, I scheduled a reflection session for the next class period to discuss what students had learned and become aware of in terms of US environmental history. One key takeaway for several of them was how many key figures emerged in the United States between the 1930s and the 1960s, and we talked for a while about what might explain that. I ended that class with a quiz that asked them to articulate their key understandings from the unit as a whole. In the end, while the class activity itself was certainly enjoyable, I wanted to make sure I could assess the degree to which they understood the material and could demonstrate some of the key learning goals I had articulated for the course as a whole. By facilitating the party, reading their papers, and grading their quizzes, I was able to get a good sense of their emerging understandings—much more so than I had in previous attempts. It wasn't perfect. "Emerson" didn't bother with a costume and his paper was a bit of a mess. "Winona LaDuke" bombed the quiz and seemed grumpy that I had made the class complete one in the first place. But it went well enough that it became a mainstay in the course.

For many faculty, assessment is perhaps the least creative and interesting element of teaching. We post complaints on Facebook during exam periods lamenting our procrastinated pile of work waiting to be graded. As young professors, we silently cringe as we hand back assessed student work and grades, waiting for the backlash of complaints and grade grubbing that inevitably comes. And, when it comes time for accreditation, we all roll our eyes as the dean or department chair comes around asking for yet another curriculum map or document about learning goals and outcomes. But one thing I have learned in my journey toward risky teaching is that risky assessment can actually be a surprisingly creative engine for pedagogical experimentation. When we begin by imagining what kinds of student work we would love to see, what products we would be excited to assess, what "presents" we would open with anticipation, we may be getting somewhere. When we consciously put in more student choice, more authentic activity, and more integration, the assessment can drive the learning in the best possible ways. Too often, we begin with the content and the course design and then figure out how we might generate grades almost as an afterthought. But taking risks as faculty doesn't just involve the activity of teaching. If we can also see the possibilities in risk-taking with assessment, we might just surprise ourselves and our students with what we can create, together. We might even consider bringing back the E grade.

REFERENCES

Association of American Colleges and Universities (AACU). (2009). *Integrative learning VALUE rubric*. Retrieved from: www.aacu.org/value/rubrics/integrative-learning

Burns, B. (2018). *Changing the culture of higher education, together*. Retrieved from: www.youtube.com/watch?v=BksG3y7S5xY

Chase, A. M., Clancy, H. A., Lachance, R. P., Mathison, B. M., Chiu, M. M., & Weaver, G. C. (2017). Improving critical thinking via authenticity: The CASPiE research experience in a military academy chemistry course. *Chemistry Education Research and Practice, 18*(1), 55–63.

Clark, H. (2015). *A culture of one right answer.* Retrieved from: www.hollyclark.org/2015/12/21/a-culture-of-one-right-answer/

Davidson, C. N. (2017). *The new education.* New York: Basic Books.

Freeman, S., Eddy, S. L., McDonough, M., Smith, M. K., Okoroafor, N., Jordt, H., & Wenderoth, M. P. (2014). Active learning increases student performance in science, engineering, and mathematics. *Proceedings of the National Academy of Sciences, 111*(23), 8410–8415.

Haake, D. C., HilleRisLambers, J., Pitre, E., & Freeman, S. (2011). Increased structure and active learning reduce the achievement gap in introductory biology. *Science, 332*(6034), 1213–1216.

Heifetz, R. A. (2009). *Leadership without easy answers.* Boston, MA: Harvard University Press.

Kapor, M. (2008). Productive failure. *Cognition and Instruction, 26*(3), 379–425.

McDermott, R. (1997). Achieving school failure: An anthropological approach to illiteracy and social stratification. In G. Spinder (Ed.), *Education and cultural process: Anthropological approaches* (pp. 173–209). Long Grove, IL: Waveland Press.

President's Council of Advisors on Science and Technology. (2012). *Engage to excel: Producing one million additional college graduates with degrees in science, technology, engineering, and mathematics.* Retrieved from: https://files.eric.ed.gov/fulltext/ED541511.pdf

Stommel, J. (2018). *How to ungrade.* Retrieved from: www.jessestommel.com/how-to-ungrade/

Supiano, B. (2019). *Grades can hinder learning.* Retrieved from: www.chronicle.com/article/grades-can-hinder-learning-what-should-professors-use-instead

Weaver, G. (2019). Personal communication.

Chapter 8
Leadership and Uncertainty

INTRODUCTION

When I proposed this book about risk and uncertainty and then began writing in the summer of 2019, there was no global pandemic on the horizon and, as I look back, it seems like an entirely different world. The scale and scope of the impact of Covid-19 are almost unimaginable. The challenges we now face in higher education involve the highest degrees of uncertainty in the modern existence of the academy. Some schools, like Paul Quinn College and the University of California system, decided that the uncertainty and the risks were too great and elected to close down in-person instruction in favor of an online curriculum only in the fall of 2020. Other universities, like Purdue University, came out almost as early to declare that they would open for in-person instruction, seeing the risks involved as a necessary part of completing their educational mission. And, no surprise, there were critics on all sides of the issue. Many saw the early fall outbreaks at several large universities as evidence that campuses had opened too soon. Others pointed out that the vast majority of schools were managing through the pandemic reasonably well and that classrooms were not the real threat—social gatherings outside campus were causing most of the issues. Regardless, the risks and uncertainty with which we wrestled in the summer of 2020 as administrators and faculty were almost comical were they not so serious. Do we need to wipe down classrooms before and after every class? How do we control traffic flow into and out of buildings to minimize exposure? Should every dorm room be a single? How do we get student athletes safely to and from sports competitions? Do returned library materials need to be quarantined? How do we socially distance and fit enough students into the cafeteria? How are we going to teach in-person and online simultaneously? And now, as we look to begin the 2021–22 school year, the delta variant has added further complexity at a time all of us were hoping for a more straightforward start to the year. We now have new challenges associated with vaccines, religious exemptions, and mandatory versus voluntary mask-wearing policies.

DOI: 10.4324/9781003029809-10

Given our current challenges, there are now risks and uncertainty that extend far beyond much of what we have discussed in this book.

I chose to make a career change right in the middle of all of this, accepting a position at Warren Wilson College in Asheville, North Carolina. Normally, such a move would be a cause for celebration at the chance to advance one's career and strike out on a new adventure. There was certainly some of that emotion as we packed up our house in Indiana and moved the whole family, including a dog, cat, rabbit, and two fish. Selling our house, purchasing one in North Carolina, and moving our household during an active pandemic was definitely an adventure. But it paled in comparison to what I found as I began my new job at Warren Wilson. In early July 2020, we were managing, simultaneously, the health concerns and decisions about Covid-19, the trauma and racial reckoning resulting from the death of George Floyd, and the economic fallout from the pandemic and from the drop in enrollment and room and board revenue. Our cabinet meetings felt more like the work of an emergency response team than a higher education leadership group. The complexity, urgency, ambiguity, and stress we were attempting to manage was unlike anything I had experienced before as a senior administrator. I remember one day in particular. It was mid-July, and we were in a "go; no-go" decision moment as to whether to open up the residence halls for the fall. This was a major call that would impact not just the budget sheet but the health and safety of our students, faculty, and staff. While we had good counsel from our regional health advisors and state public health officials, there was a lot we simply did not and could not know. What if we open to in-person instruction and then have to close again? Could we afford to give room and board refunds? What if we have an outbreak that overwhelms our quarantine spaces? What if someone gets seriously ill? What if someone dies? It was a somber discussion made all the more surreal by the fact that we were not meeting in person—we could only look at each other through a computer screen as we attempted to make what would be one of the biggest calls of our professional lives. As we discussed the pros and cons of various possibilities, I kept thinking back on the VUCA principle introduced earlier in this book. We were living through a classic VUCA scenario—a volatile, uncertain, complex, and ambiguous situation. How were we going to navigate our way through this?

Much of this book has been about how we can enhance and celebrate risk-taking and uncertainty in and out of the classroom in higher education. I must admit, as I write this concluding chapter, I wonder if the message of this book is now a bit out of tune. Don't we already have enough uncertainty? Who, at this moment, wants to think about taking more risks and designing for more uncertainty? All of us could stand for a little more stability in our lives—like the simple act of heading out the door to grab a bite to eat at a local restaurant. Or teaching a class without a mask. We yearn for the support and comfort of a simple hug.

These are taken-for-granted experiences in our day-to-day lives that have been disrupted, and, as a result, we all wish for a return to something close to normal.

But, the etymology of the word crisis has within it the notion of a decision, of a turning point, and, thus, opportunity. Rahm Emanuel, President Obama's chief of staff, once remarked, "never let a crisis go to waste." There may always be a certain cynicism about this idea—who gets to decide how we "use" a crisis? Who benefits? Who takes on the burden? But there is a simple truth in seeing a crisis as a decisive moment, as a potential turning point, as an opportunity to do things differently. Across higher education, innovation already has been born from necessity. Schools that had long ignored online learning have been forced to scale up. Faculty who refused to use the learning management system suddenly found themselves relying on it to deliver instruction. Staff and administrators had to quickly learn new workflows that did not involve "pushing paper," but rather relied on technology to get work done. And, as it turns out, some of these forced changes were for the good. We learned that working from home was not, inevitably, unproductive. We learned that you could, in fact, build community in online classrooms. We learned that the pace of reform as it relates to racial justice on our campuses was insufficient. And we relearned that our students are powerful agents for change.

So, while all of us could use a little less uncertainty and risk-taking in our daily lives, there is an upside. How can we use this moment to respond in real, material ways to the underlying issues brought to the surface by these crises? This book has asked how we can, as faculty and staff, work with our students to embrace uncertainty and productive risk-taking. We should also be exploring how our institutional leaders and our colleges and universities as a whole might embrace more uncertainty and productive risk-taking as well. While the temptation may be just to "get through it" so that we can then get back to normal, there is good reason to believe that we never will get back to that old version of normal. Some of the resets we are experiencing now will remain permanent—this is certainly going to be the case with online learning. Even the most staunchly in-person, residential colleges will likely continue to develop more hybrid and online options in a post-pandemic world. As Kasia Lundy writes,

> The past 16 months have been particularly difficult for institutions of higher education, but, in many cases, the difficult circumstances have provided a once-in-a-lifetime opportunity to spur change on campuses. The institutions that have quickly pivoted and made difficult decisions will likely be in a stronger position coming out of the pandemic. The key is to now continue to transform to face the future. Institution leaders who were able to take advantage of opportunities during the pandemic are now grappling with the question of how they can maintain momentum coming out of the pandemic.

> Maintaining the appetite for strategic change can be critical moving forward because institutions that do not take the opportunity to transform during this period will be especially vulnerable to the challenges ahead.
>
> (Lundy, 2021)

What might it look like for institutions and institutional leaders (not just faculty and students) to fully embrace uncertainty and productive risk-taking coming out of this period? Much of the following discussion comes from my own experiences in leadership in higher education at several institutions, in addition to interviews with, observations of, and interactions I have had with senior leaders over my Fellowship year with the American Council of Education and in completing research for this book. Almost all of what I share I do so with great humility. The lessons outlined in this chapter come from experiences I have had—often experiences with failure. There is an old story about the hiring of a new senior leader on campus who came from another institution. The search committee decided on experience as opposed to an up-and-coming candidate. When asked why, the chair remarked, "Because we wanted someone who made her mistakes somewhere else before she came here!" There is some sense in that. Yet it is also true that we continue to make mistakes (hopefully different ones) throughout our professional lives. The impact of those mistakes just tends to be more far-reaching and influential as we grow in our careers if we are one of the "lucky" ones who move from the classroom to administration. And actually, many of the same teaching principles discussed in this book apply quite readily to the senior leader and to the institution as a whole. It just takes on a slightly different approach. I remember a former president at Earlham, Doug Bennett, who sat me down once when I said I didn't think I wanted to be an administrator because I liked teaching too much. He said, "Jay, you don't stop being a teacher when you move to administration. It's just a different form of teaching." Fifteen years on from that talk, I understand more and more what he was saying.

FUNDAMENTAL PRINCIPLES OF LEADING THROUGH UNCERTAINTY

What follows are principles for leading through uncertainty. I believe they are applicable to every style and form of leadership we might think of in higher education. Whether you are a department chair, a program director, an academic dean, or a senior leader, we all wrestle with complexity and uncertainty in our jobs. And, in fact, if we think about leadership beyond the old paradigm of a single individual "in charge" of others, every person working in the organization leads in their own way. So, these principles can really apply to everyone on campus. They are my principles and, as such, may not resonate with every person and every leadership context. They are born from my own experience.

Nonetheless, my hope is that each reader will be able to find useful elements that resonate.

START WITH THE WHY

During one particularly intense round of planning and change at my former institution, the committee I was chairing entertained a significant shift to the academic calendar (we were on semesters at the time). We launched into various models and permutations of embedded January terms and the like and held a series of meetings and discussions in the community. I recall one meeting, when we were stuck in the proverbial weeds of the details around what this new calendar would look like at the practical level of the daily-weekly schedule, a faculty member threw up his hands and said with clear exasperation in his voice, "Can somebody please tell me again why we are trying to change the calendar?!"

Simon Sinek, in his book *Start With Why*, refers to the "golden circle" when it comes to how organizations and businesses motivate people. In this model, the first and central circle is the Why, the next circle around the Why is the How, and the final circle around both the Why and the How is the What. To Sinek, most companies and organizations can easily articulate their What: in essence, what products or services they provide. Many businesses can also articulate their How—the ways they provide their What in a manner that is distinctive or demonstrably better than the competition. But to Sinek,

> Very few people or companies can clearly describe WHY they do WHAT they do. When I say WHY, I don't mean to make money—that's a result. By WHY I mean what is your purpose, cause, or belief? WHY does your company exist? ... And WHY should anyone care?
>
> (Sinek, 2011, p. 39)

While Sinek is writing for a corporate audience, the idea of starting with Why applies equally to higher education. As for the calendar change and the exasperated faculty member, we had spent quite a bit of time on the What and the How of the proposed changes, but we missed emphasizing the Why. While we had talked with the community about the reasons for a new calendar early on, we assumed, erroneously, that it was now clear to everyone as we discussed the details of implementation.

Institutions and institutional leaders can help groups and communities manage uncertainty and take productive risks by ensuring that everyone is clear on the purpose of the endeavor. In times of uncertainty, we need to focus on the Why even as the What and the How pull at our attention. More than just the issuing of emails and one-way institutional communications, real and deep investment in the Why actually involves a continual process of listening and discussion, articulation and rearticulation with our community members. I recall one college president I spoke with talk about the discipline of repetition. I watched this president move between a variety of community stakeholder groups over the course of a particular day. With each separate audience, he would repeat the same three strategic imperatives the institution was working on, giving a short, high-level description of each. At the end of the day, I asked him about how he can manage to say the same thing so many times and still make it sound fresh. He remarked,

> it may not be new to me, but I have to remember that it may be new to the audience I am speaking with. If you are sick and tired of repeating the institutional goals and objectives in your public talks, you probably have said them just about enough times.

BE STILL

It can be tempting, during periods of uncertainty, as a leader to just focus on action and decision-making. After all, this is a dominant stereotype of strong leadership—a single individual taking bold and decisive action. But first responders, individuals who deal with highly stressful, chaotic, crisis environments, are trained to do something called a "scene survey" first before they begin to administer aid. The scene survey does several things. First, it ensures that the rescuer does not become another person to be rescued by stumbling into the same environment that got the person or persons injured in the first place. This is unfortunately all too common in situations like drownings and car accidents. Second, a survey of the scene gives the first responder a chance to calm down, take several deep breaths, and analyze what they see. Without this crucial step, a rescuer could miss important details and information. This can be incredibly hard to do when every fiber of your being wants to jump into action and help.

The recent Black Lives Matter and racial justice movement is a case in point. After the multiple disturbing events of racial violence that occurred over the summer of 2020, we at Warren Wilson, like many institutions and leaders, sensed that, this time, something was different. We could see, hear, and feel the upset in our students, our alumni, and our community of faculty and staff. It was clear that we had to do something and quickly. So, we got together as a leadership team, discussed the situation, and then agreed that our president should write a letter and send it out. Which she did. It was a wonderful letter. Heartfelt, personal, and reflective not only of her own position and identity as a White woman in the United States but also of the needed and necessary improvements for the college as it related to our students and faculty of color. Many other presidents and institutions did the same. Almost instantly, it was clear that these letters were a mistake. The communications struck many in the higher education community, and in particular our students of color, as disingenuous, tone-deaf, and shallow.

At Warren Wilson, it was also quickly pointed out that, in our haste to "do something," we had failed to include a single person of color in the collaboration and decision to write a letter about this particular moment of racial reckoning. We were justifiably criticized for our approach and our ignorance, and it was a humbling moment. In our rush to just do something, we forgot to do a scene survey and take a breath. As a result, we missed important details.

To be still, from an institutional leadership point of view, means focusing on process first, before jumping into action. It means making sure you have the right people in the room for decision-making. Beyond just crisis management, it means investing in your people, their ideas, and their perspectives. This inevitably takes time, which is often the one thing you don't believe you have. But time stress is a funny thing. It can distort your perception of decision-making and make you feel as though you have to be hasty, when often you really don't. The old saw is: "If you want to go fast, go alone. But if you want to go far, go together." In wilderness guiding scenarios, going fast can often get you and those you are caring for injured or killed. Guides are trained to purposefully slow down when circumstances get increasingly complex, uncertain, and risky. The same is true in higher education. More times than I care to admit, I have justified going fast and alone under the false assumption that, "we don't have time for more consultation." But, in hindsight, I almost always had the time and, paradoxically, by not taking a moment to be still, I wound up spending more time and more resources cleaning up mistakes after the fact.

To be still when it comes to uncertainty and taking risks as an institutional leader often involves asking such questions as the following:

What is the problem we are trying to solve here?
What data do we need and how do we get it?
Who decides and by what process?
What are our timelines?
What interim checkpoints need to be established?
Who needs to be consulted? At what points in the process?
What is the final outcome we are trying to achieve?
What does success look like?
What metrics and key performance indicators would tell us we are on track or off track?

To be still also means resisting going to the "same ten people" (STPs) to launch an initiative or form a working group. We go for the STPs because it is easier and faster. They are reliable, we like them, and we know what to expect in terms of their work output and their commitment to the enterprise. But, in sticking with that particular habit, we lose a tremendous opportunity to grow the pool of individuals who are interested and invested in the work. Worse, it can breed resentment and cynicism as the rest of the community looks on as the same ten people are chosen, yet again, for service on the committee. The temptation in leadership is to sideline the cynics, the critics, and the skeptics. But, more often than not, you need those people on the team. In my experience, many of these folks ask just the right questions during ideation that sharpen the mind and the end product. And, these folks are going to be asking these questions and making the criticisms anyway. Better to have them engaged early than right before a faculty deliberation and vote, for example.

CHANGE AND THE ENEMY OF THE GOOD

As we have discussed throughout this book, learning requires failure. We don't learn how to ride a bike without falling off from time to time. We don't learn how to write a good essay without writing what Anne Lamott called "shitty first drafts" (2007) along the way. Yet, all throughout our institutions there exists a fear of failure. The perfect becomes the enemy of the good. We aim for perfect proposals, perfect educational models, and perfect initiatives, and we spend inordinate amounts of time behind closed doors perfecting our perfect proposals before we dare submit them to public scrutiny. Of course, this is also what we teach our students in many ways as they work on their "one and done" papers. We are perfectionists because we don't want to lose face in front of our fellow (really smart) faculty and staff members. Colleges and universities can also exhibit perfectionism as they obsess over reputational status. When planning for a new initiative, there is the inevitable question: "Well, what is [institution X] doing?" We pour over "overlap" schools and aspirational schools to compare ourselves. And we try very hard to stick out and be distinctive. And the thing underneath all of it that keeps us up at night is fear. A fear of losing face and reputational status and a fear of failure.

But all this comes at quite a cost. Good ideas die on the vine because we don't want to risk our hard-earned reputation or lose places in the rankings. Innovators on our campuses are dismissed before they have a chance to implement ideas. The killer phrases come out the second something new or different is floated: "We already tried that and it didn't work last time;" "we need a committee to investigate that;" "let's be realistic;" "we don't want to look foolish." But the irony is, we also look with jealous eyes at those institutions who have taken risks and succeeded. If we could just guarantee that our risk-taking would be successful, we would do it. But, that's the thing with risk—we don't know if what we are attempting will work. We have to put some real skin in the game. Once, while home on a break from college, I had an argument with my father. I described myself to him as a risk-taker, and he wasn't so sure. To prove him wrong (and what 20-year-old home from college doesn't want to prove his parents wrong?), I cited my recent skydiving adventure. "But Jay," my Dad said, "that really wasn't taking a risk. You already knew you could do it before you attempted it. A risk is trying something you aren't sure will work." Putting aside the notion that when things don't work while skydiving, there are dire consequences, I understood his point. While skydiving made me somewhat nervous and uncomfortable, I didn't really think I would turn away from the challenge once I got on that plane. If we know we can do something successfully, it is not really a risk.

And this brings us to failure. Innovation, like learning, often requires failure. In an entrepreneurial sense, what we are after is "failing fast, failing cheap, and failing forward." There is a tendency in higher education to design and overengineer initiatives to death. We aim to develop the "immaculate curriculum," perfect in all ways and in all times. We try to work out all the bugs and kinks before we launch something. And, this makes logical sense. In education, we are not producing widgets or apps. There are long-term consequences when we change general education, for example. We have to track students, assess learning outcomes, and change graduation requirements and faculty loads. These are not small things, and we are wise to think it through carefully and completely. Yet there is also a downside risk to our "paralysis by analysis" in higher education and to our culture of fear of failure. Our current structures in higher education are struggling to respond to the moment in a variety of ways. As Jeff Selingo writes, "Change comes very slowly to higher education. A confluence of events—flagging state support for public colleges, huge federal budget deficits, and falling household income—now make it necessary to consider new approaches" (Selingo, 2019, p. xviii). Selingo goes on to argue,

> American higher education is broken. Like another American icon—the auto industry in Detroit—the higher education industry is beset by hubris, opposition to change, and resistance to accountability. Even the leaders of colleges and universities think we are in trouble. More than one-third of them say American higher education is heading in the wrong direction.
>
> (Ibid, p. xviii)

And all of this was written before the global pandemic. Whether or not you share Selingo's pessimism about the pace of change in the sector, few would deny that the pressures and strains on higher education are at a fever pitch and risk is unavoidable.

And we do have examples of colleges and universities that are overcoming the fear of failure while successfully attempting risky things. I have a former ACE colleague who worked with a President and Cabinet at a large public university known for innovation who commented on the culture there. "Things just move

141

faster," she recalled. "It's like they are used to having new initiatives coming forward and they focus on keeping them moving. When something isn't working, the project leaders don't panic, they just work on retooling it. They are really breaking away from the rigidity of 'we've been doing it this way for years.' The culture encourages and supports new ideas." My colleague also noted that the culture there is integrated all the way down to new faculty. "I sat in on new faculty orientation and I asked many of them 'what drew you to work for this institution?' Many of them didn't know a lot about the university because they were brand new to the institution, but they all said what drew them was this possibility for newness, this possibility for change and innovating—doing something different and unexpected."

But importantly, my colleague also noted that innovation and risk taking does have its downsides. "I also talked to people there who brought up the issue of innovation fatigue. This idea that always chasing after the next, new thing, can be tiring. I remember I interviewed one faculty member who said, 'You know, just because we can do something doesn't mean that we should.'"

Getting the balance right between encouraging a culture of innovation and risk-taking while supporting longstanding institutional norms, values, and identity is where leadership becomes critical. Freeman Hrabowski, president at the University of Maryland Baltimore County (UMBC), has become a national figure in the higher education reform movement for the astonishing gains and outcomes he has overseen at UMBC. In his book *The Empowered University*, he has a chapter titled "Culture Change is Hard as Hell," which highlights the ways in which culture change is both a series of small steps and tectonic shifts.

> Culture change does not happen all at once. It can be almost imperceptible at times. One person gets it, then another, and then another. And then one day you sense that it has happened and that the tipping point has been crossed. These successes had altered our beliefs as a community about what is possible. They had altered our values. We had embraced inclusive excellence, student success, and innovation.
>
> (2019, p. 171)

In a very real sense, the same small ball approach to teaching innovation that we discussed in Chapter 5 applies to thinking about risk and change at the senior leader and institutional levels. Swinging for the fences is often what we think of when it comes to risk-taking and innovation. We are told that, in order to innovate, organizations need to "reinvent themselves" or pivot in some extreme and dramatic fashion. Perhaps. But, just as often, the successful risky leader and risky institution look a whole lot more like what President Hrabowski describes—a range of seemingly minor and small shifts that, when taken together, represent a profound shift in thinking and action.

IT IS ALL ABOUT RELATIONSHIPS

Parker Palmer once wrote, "Technique is what teachers use until the real teacher arrives" (Palmer, 2007, p. 5). The same is true for leadership. Authentic leadership is hard to define and describe but clear to see when it is missing. But a significant component of authenticity is relationships. Folks want to know who you are and that you care, before they want to know about the latest idea, innovation, or initiative you hope to launch. Jerome Murphy, author of *Dancing in the Rain* and former dean at the Harvard Graduate School of Education, uses the acronym of MYDANCE to articulate what it means to lead from a place of authenticity and relationship.

> Mind your values: Take action inspired by what matters most to you
> Yield to now: Slow down and focus your attention on the present moment
> Disentangle from upsets: Mentally step back . . . from upsets [rather than] . . . overidentifying with them
> Allow unease: Open up to upsets even if you dislike them
> Nourish yourself: Engage in everyday activities designed to replenish your energy
> Cherish self-compassion: Give yourself the kindness you need and deserve
> Express feelings wisely: Carefully reveal your human side to build trust
> (Murphy, 2019, p. 9)

What Murphy is getting at, and what I believe is crucial to acknowledge when we are leading with and through uncertainty, is the idea of relational leadership. Related to the well-known concept of emotional intelligence, relational leadership is the manifestation of emotional intelligence within a given leadership context. John Mayer, one of early proponents of the term, states, "[f]rom a scientific (rather than a popular) standpoint, emotional intelligence is the ability to accurately perceive your own and others' emotions; to understand the signals that emotions send about relationships; and to manage your own and others' emotions" (Mayer, Goleman, Barrett, & Gutstein, 2004). Leading through uncertainty and asking individuals, teams, and institutions to take risks are an inherently emotional exercise. Chip and Dan Heath, the authors of *Switch: How to change things when change is hard*, use the analogy of the elephant and the rider. The rider is our cognitive or rational brain—the one that can see and understand the world through the lens of reason, data, and evidence. The elephant is the emotional brain—the part that needs to feel supported, encouraged, and prepared to move through a world that can appear uncertain and even scary. They argue that we cannot just manage and lead change from the perspective of the rider, we have to also consider the elephant. "What looks like laziness is often exhaustion. The Rider can't get his way by force for very long. So it's critical that you engage people's emotional side—get their Elephants on the path" (Heath & Heath, 2010, p. 17).

Throughout my career in higher education, I have watched good ideas and productively risky innovations fall by the wayside because the relational components of change were not adequately addressed. One year, a new dean declared that our system for study abroad would have to change—this, at an institution known for international education where faculty organized and led almost all of the trips rather than outsourcing them to third-party providers or direct enrollment through international universities. The model was expensive and, in a sense, "inefficient." The rider side of the brain knew this to be true. But we also had a history of faculty-led study abroad that was a tremendous success and something the community was justifiably proud of—the elephant side of the brain knew this to be true as well. This all came to a head one day when the new dean called a meeting of just a few key faculty and administrators to explore the idea of shifting our system to a different model. Word got around campus that this meeting was taking place and, when the dean walked into the meeting, it was standing room only—packed with faculty (and elephants) ready to defend and fight for the current system. I think the dean learned an important lesson that day about the relational side of change when considering new ideas or initiatives.

Of course, it is easy to judge and criticize other leaders in hindsight. I have learned my own hard lessons about relational leadership as well. When I first arrived at Warren Wilson as the new Vice President for Academic Affairs, it was right in the middle of the pandemic. In addition to the usual business of managing a college, which would be challenging enough on a good day, I walked into an environment where the perceived levels of risk and uncertainty were heightened to the extreme. To add to the surreal quality of those early months, the entirety of my interactions with the community were through the computer screen, making it difficult to get a sense of the campus and the people I was supposed to lead and serve. One day, in cabinet, as we were working our way through a range of complex and challenging decisions about reopening the college in the fall, a relatively minor issue was brought up: should we allow the children of faculty and staff on campus since it will be closed? As a small, community-oriented school, Warren Wilson faculty and staff were accustomed to bringing their kids to work for one reason or another, and this was always allowed. But in the midst of a pandemic where we were trying to control a virus, it seemed like the right and logical thing to do to ask faculty and staff to have their children remain off-campus until the threat was over. I remember not giving it much thought in cabinet at the time, and we quickly decided to establish this new "policy" and directed human resources to send out an email. Within hours of that email going out, my in-box was flooded with upset and angry community members. "How could you?" many of them said. "In the midst of everything, with all the challenges we are having to deal with, you decide to ban children from campus!?" We were accused of being antifamily, of a lack of consultation and collaboration, and, in general, of just being idiots. And, I have to say, the community was right. We had missed both the practical side and the emotional side of the issue. What we thought, as leaders, was, "this makes sense to do." What the community heard was, "we don't care about you." It took many meetings and some serious humble pie eating to make things right again, and I learned, once again, about the power of relational leadership.

CONCLUSION: THE ANTIFRAGILE LEADER AND INSTITUTION

Nassim Talib, author of the book *Antifragile: Things That Gain from Disorder*, writes,

> Some things benefit from shocks; they thrive and grow when exposed to volatility, randomness, disorder, and stressors and love adventure, risk, and uncertainty. Yet, in spite of the ubiquity of the phenomenon, there is no word for the exact opposite of fragile. Let us call it antifragile. Antifragility is beyond resilience or robustness. The resilient resists shocks and stays the same; the antifragile gets better. This property is behind everything that has changed with time: evolution, culture, ideas, revolutions, political systems, technological innovation, cultural and economic success, corporate survival, good recipes (say, chicken soup or steak tartare with a drop of cognac), the rise of cities, cultures, legal systems, equatorial forests, bacterial resistance . . . even our own existence as a species on this planet.
>
> The antifragile loves randomness and uncertainty, which also means— crucially—a love of errors, a certain class of errors. Antifragility has a singular property of allowing us to deal with the unknown, to do things without understanding them— and do them well. Let me be more aggressive: we are largely better at doing than we are at thinking, thanks to antifragility. I'd rather be dumb and antifragile than extremely smart and fragile, any time.
>
> (Talib, 2020)

Talib aptly sums up the qualities we have been talking about throughout this book: how teachers, students, and academic leaders can embrace uncertainty and learn to work with it to further educational and institutional outcomes. He is right to point out that we struggle to describe this quality in a single word. Grit and resilience are often used. Innovation and entrepreneurialism describe elements of it. Adaptation and nimbleness offer one way to frame the qualities we are after. Yet, as Talib writes, none of them address the idea of not just dealing with uncertainty but embracing it. The term "antifragile" is Talib's attempt to codify this stance. It's an awkward term and perhaps not quite on the mark for daily usage. But his overall point is spot-on. How can we, as Talib writes, "deal with the unknown, to do things without understanding them—and do them well." That last part is the crucial part—how do we deal with uncertainty successfully? How can we not just survive in uncertainty, but thrive? How can we use the qualities of uncertainty to advance, achieve, and succeed?

I have framed this book around the idea of risky teaching to describe how we might use uncertainty to achieve in the way Talib describes. Yet working with uncertainty in this way is rarely discussed in academia. It is as if risk and the attendant issues of uncertainty, doubt, and failure are things we just don't want to talk about when it comes to our institutions, our classrooms, and ourselves. Yet, there are traditions, often spiritual and religious traditions, that can point the way to why walking in and through the shadow times are a necessary part of a process of transformation. Richard Rohr writes,

> It seems a movement from certitude to doubt and through doubt to acceptance of life's mystery is necessary in all encounters, intellectual breakthroughs, and relationships, not just with the Divine. . . . To know anything fully is always to hold that part of it which is still mysterious and unknowable. Our youthful demand for certainty does eliminate most anxiety on the conscious level, so I can see why many of us stay in such a control tower during the first half of life. We are too fragile yet.
>
> (Rohr, 2020)

Rohr goes on the cite author Sue Monk Kidd, who wonders,

> What has happened to our ability to dwell in unknowing, to live inside a question and coexist with the tensions of uncertainty? Where is our willingness to incubate pain and let it birth something new? What has happened to patient unfolding, to endurance? These things are what form the ground of waiting. And if you look carefully, you'll see that they're also the seedbed of creativity and growth—what allows us to do the daring and to break through to newness.
>
> (Ibid, 2020)

Higher education in the United States and throughout the world is under a great deal of strain. Some might even say that the sector is "too fragile" in the way Rohr describes and is in the process of breaking apart as the model that has existed for centuries finally reaches the limits of its usefulness and effectiveness. There are good reasons to be pessimistic about the future of the academy. Yet, the death of the university, or the liberal arts, has been predicted many times. Is this time different? Perhaps. Kidd reminds us that sitting with uncertainty and doubt can actually lead us to a place of daring, newness, and rebirth. Whether or not the doomsday prognostications are accurate, what is clear is that our institutions, our classrooms, and our academic leaders would do well to embrace uncertainty and design in the qualities of antifragility that Talib identifies. This will not just serve our institutions but, importantly, it will better serve our students who will have to graduate into this world of challenges and wicked problems.

There have been so many times in my teaching career when I was filled with doubt. Self-doubt, doubt about a particular class or activity I was planning, doubt about the subject matter. As I grew in my career and became an administrator, those doubts never left me. They just took on a different hue and dimension. The temptation to turn away from doubt and toward the perceived security of certainty is always present. But this often involves some form of defensive crouch. And the paradox of it all is, when we do this, it often generates the very outcome we most fear. To take a risk when all is uncertain and when the snarling dogs of doubt snap at your heels is perhaps the hardest thing to do—as a person, as a teacher, as a leader, and as an institution. You could fail. You could fall on your face. You could do real harm to others. It is important to acknowledge all of that. Yet, there are also many examples of individuals and organizations using these moments of doubt and uncertainty as a catalyst for transformation. My enduring hope for higher education, for all who work in it, for faculty, for staff, and for students is that we respond to this moment with courage, with integrity, and with grace. Uncertainty will always be among us. The fundamental question is: how shall we work with it?

REFERENCES

Heath, C., & Heath, D. (2010). *Switch*. New York: Broadway Books.

Hrabowski, F. (2019). *The empowered university*. Baltimore, MD: Johns Hopkins Press.

Lamott, A. (2007). *Bird by bird*. Norwell, MA: Anchor Press.

Lundy, K. (2021). *Seizing the moment*. Retrieved from: https://www.insidehighered.com/views/2021/06/25/colleges-should-use-recovery-funds-rethink-how-they-operate-opinion

Mayer, J. D., Goleman, D., Barrett, C., & Gutstein, S. (2004). Leading by feel. *Harvard Business Review, 82*(1), 27.

Murphy, J. T. (2019). *Dancing in the rain*. Boston, MA: Harvard Education Press.

Palmer, P. J. (2007). *The courage to teach*. New York: John Wiley & Sons.

Rohr, R. (2020). *Faith and doubt are not opposites*. Retrieved February 12, 2020, from: https://cac.org/faith-and-doubt-are-not-opposites-2021-02-03/

Seltzer, R. (2020). College leadership in an era of unpredictability. *Inside Higher Education Special Report*. Washington, DC. Retrieved from: https://www.insidehighered.com/content/college-leadership-era-unpredictability

Sinek, S. (2011). *Start with why*. New York: Penguin Press.

Talib, N. (2020). *Antifragile: A definition*. Retrieved January 10, 2020, from: https://fs.blog/2014/04/antifragile-a-definition/

Index

Note: Page numbers in italics indicate a figure on the corresponding page.

2016 Hult Prize competition: goals of 28; Team Magic Bus 28–30

academic disciplines, economic reorientation impact on 22
ACE *see* American Council on Education
active and game-based learning 12
active learning: component 85; designs 116; exercise 130; *vs.* passive learning 79–80; student response to 49–50
activity trap 110
"administrative bloat" argument 47
administrators 24, 28–9, 36–7, 41, 46–7, 133, 135–6, 144, 147
Alabama Department of Transportation 78
Albrecht, Karl 65–6
ALDOT *see* Alabama Department of Transportation
"alternative campus tour" 103
American Council on Education 25
Amirkhanian, Armen 77–9, 81, 95
antifragility 145–7
anti-racist workshop 13
anxiety 31, 51, 146
Appell, Elizabeth 95
"arming behaviors" 71
armored leadership 71–2
assessments 61, 84–5, 93, 115–16, 125–8, 130–1; "culture of one right answer" 119; by design 120; designing for risky 119–21; failure 117–19; formative 122–3; student assignments 119; summative 122; *see also* grading; risky assessment; "ungrading"
assignments 58–9, 61, 68, 70, 88, 91–4, 110, 116, 123–8; creative 120; experiential 69, 92; high-stakes 121; nontraditional 93; reflection 120
assumptions, about teacher 4–5
audience 6–7, 46, 126, 138; authentic 29–30, 121; corporate 137
authenticity 126–7, 143; and audience 126–7; and relationship, lead from place of 143–4
authentic leadership 143

backwards design 84
"banking method" of education 50
Bass, Randy 29, 46
Bear Stearns 19
Big, Meaningful, Audacious Goal 69, 84, 93
Black Lives Matter (BLM) movement 18, 138–9
blaming 71
BMAG *see* Big, Meaningful, Audacious Goal
Boiling Frog concept 90–2, 95
"bounded choice" 123
Bow and the Arrow concept 89–90
brain response 52, 91
brainstorm 87, 94
brave spaces 50, 52–3, 52–4
"broccoli dilemma" 47–50
Brown, Brené 71–2
bureaucratization of education 115
Burns, Bridgette 39, 41, 117
Busteed, Brandon 20–1

149

INDEX

capstone project 57; *see also* playground project
career 3–4, 12, 37–8, 44, 63, 66, 89, 93, 104, 127–8, 134, 136, 144, 147
CASPiE *see* Center for Authentic Science Practice in Education
Center for Authentic Science Practice in Education 127
Center for Entrepreneurship and Innovation 29
Chödrön, Pema 14, 71
Chronicle of Higher Education 80
classroom community, facilitating 90
climate change 33
Clinton, Bill 28
Clinton Foundation 27
cognitive maps 17
collaboration 29, 43, 49, 57, 102, 139, 145
collaborative course design 86–7
college: choice drivers, for Generation Z 40; college-going population, demographic drop in 27; degree, new pathway for getting 20–1; experience and workplace engagement, link between 43–4; professorship 13; ranking systems, parameters for 21
communities: as classrooms 102–3; capacity building 102; engagement 93, 98
community-based learning 42, 98
community-engaged learning 79, 102–3
community-engaged research projects 12
competence 54, 67, 89, 101, 112
competition 28–9, 137
computer and information sciences, decline in number of degrees in 22
concrete materials, learning about 77; challenges of 78; "experience before label" approach 77; "make me concrete" approach 78, 81; recipe-based approach 77
concrete mixing lab 77–9, 81, 86, 95
conservative organizational structures 47
content-level experts 5
contingent faculty member 67
"Continue-Start-Stop" exercise 90
control, in pedagogical sense 58; Dewey's framework of 58–9; relational and interdependent sense of 59; social dynamics of 58; *see also* risky teaching
"co-op" model 98
costs 6, 20–2, 25, 40–1, 51, 112, 140
counseling psychology course 92–3
courage 5, 66, 71, 106
Courage to Teach, The (Parker) 5, 66

course-based undergraduate research experience 127
course design, for uncertainty 13–14, 39, 45, 47, 58, 61, 68, 77–9, 83, 93–6, 95, 103, 120, 141, 147; backwards design 84; collaborative 86–7; "experience before label" 86; integrated design 84–6; relevance, challenge, and integration issues 92–3; time management in 93–4
course evaluations 6, 66–7, 70
course grades 115–16
course redesign 58, 69, 77–8, 81; Concrete Materials 77–9, 81; goal of 69; off-campus experience 69–70; Teagle project 69
Covid-19 global pandemic 7, 18, 25, 30, 101, 129, 141, 144; career change in middle of 134; challenges of 18, 133; as opportunity to spur change 135–6; teaching and learning experience in 7, 25, 101, 133–4, 135; uncertainty of 9, 19; as wicked problem 30–1; working from home in 135
creative assignments 120–1
creative writing pedagogy 126
culture 10, 47, 64, 102–3, 123, 141–2, 145
culture change 140–3
"culture of one right answer" 119
CURE *see* course-based undergraduate research experience
curriculum 25, 29, 58, 62, 84, 98, 103, 110, 127–9; formal 45–7; place-based 13

Dare to Lead (Brown) 71
daring leadership 71–2
data governance 121
data-information-knowledge-wisdom learning continuum 25
Davidson, Cathy 24–6, 32, 116–17
Deibel, Mike 99–101
democratic engagement 112
demographic reorientation, in higher education 25–7, 39; drop in college-going population 27; new generation of students 40–1; non-White student population 26–7, 40; population growth 26; population shifts 26
Designing the New American University (Crow)
Dewey, John 4, 30, 58–9, 86, 108
DFW rates, examination of 115–16, 127
digital skills 25

150

INDEX

direct instruction 80
disciplinary *vs.* interdisciplinary knowledge 63
disruption 19, 21, 26–7, 33
distress, physiological responses to 91
diversity 42, 50, 80, 87, 118

Earlham College 13–14, 27–8, 69, 99–101, 129, 136
Earlham Program for an Integrated Curriculum 28
economic reorientation, in higher education: academic disciplines 22–3; decline in state funding 21; Great Recession causing 19–20; new pathway for college degree 20–1; rising tuition fees 21; student debt 20; value proposition 21–2
educationally purposeful tasks 42
education *vs.* training 37
educative frame for learning 108
"edutainment" 48–9, 80
ego death, Albrecht's description of 66
Emanuel, Rahm 135
emotional intelligence 143
emotions 52, 71, 105, 129, 134, 143
endowment, Great Recession's impact on 20
"engaged pedagogy" 48
engagement 10, 12, 14, 18, 58, 68, 82, 91, 93, 95, 98, 100, 102–3, 108–9, 124, 130
enrollments, economic reorientation impact on 22
environmental studies, course for 13
EPIC *see* Earlham Program for an Integrated Curriculum
epistemological uncertainty 62
equity 50, 87, 119
eustress, physiological responses to 91
evidence-based practices 12
expectations 39, 64, 88–90, 94, 125
"experience before label" approach 77, 86
experiences 3, 10, 12–13, 16–17, 22, 27, 31, 36, 39, 42–3, 52, 57–8, 69, 71, 77–80, 83–7, 89–91, 100–11, 118, 125, 127–9, 136, 140; faculty 62–3, 64–7, 73; learning 7, 29, 45, 59, 67, 101–2, 106, 108; *see also* student experiences
experiential co-curriculum 46
experiential learning 46, 77, 79, 81–2

facilitation of uncertain learning 95; Boiling Frog concept 90–2, 95; Bow and the Arrow concept 89–90; challenges in 87; mitigating negative frames for 88; relationship building 88, 90; relevance, challenge, and integration issues 92–3; Theirs-Ours-Theirs model 88–9; time management in 93–4; *see also* risky teaching
faculty 7–8, 11, 18, 24–5, 28–30, 37, 39, 41, 45–8, 51–2, 54, 58, 81, 83–4, 86, 97–101, 105, 110, 112, 115, 117, 119–20, 123, 125, 128–9, 133–6, 138, 140, 144, 147; development 12, 64, 77, 79; experiences of 62–3, 64–7, 73; questioning taken-for-granted language 80; role in senior capstone project 57; and students experience, balance between 59
faculty-student research group 6–7
failing grade 117
Fannie Mae 19
FDS *see* First Destination Survey
fear 5, 8, 50, 62, 64–6, 70–73, 140, 147; cycle of 67–8; of failure 64, 70, 117–19, 140–1; of judgment 67; of taking risk 65; types of 65
fearful teacher 64–8
feedback 50, 84–6, 88, 90, 110, 119, 122, 125–6, 130; graded 94; iterative 93, 115; just-in-time 123
field placements 43
Fink, Dee 85–6
First Destination Survey 21
flight or fight response 52, 91
Floyd, George 18
formal curriculum 45–6
formal teaching environments 29
formative assessment 122, 123
frame 9, 11, 17, 63, 71, 108, 123–4, 145
framing of out-of-classroom learning 108–9
Freddie Mac 19
"Full Value Contract" exercise 90

Gallup-Purdue Index study 43–5
game-based learning 12, 79
garbage in, garbage out 120
Gates, Bill 23
Geertz, Clifford 112
general education 47–8, 86, 128, 141
generation Z: attitudes and preferences 40; basic traits of 40; drivers of college choice for 40
"golden circle" 137

151

INDEX

golden rule of education 41
"good enough" parent, concept of 51
"grade grubbing" 125
grades 45–6, 60–1, 66, 93, 115–17, 119–20, 122–3, 125
grading 13, 46, 93, 115–16, 118–22, 126; and assignment approach 119, 122–3; controversy 117; faculty rejecting 119; history in US 116–17
Grawe, Nathan 26–7
"Great Disruption" 18
Great Lakes College Association 63
Great Recession of 2008 19–22, 26, 37
Gruenwald, David 112

Heifetz, Ronald 123–4
herd immunity 19
higher education 8, 10–13, 16–27, 29–31, 36–7, 40–1, 43–7, 64, 67, 71, 79–80, 83, 86, 98–9, 101, 112, 115, 117–19, 122–3, 133–7, 139, 141, 144, 146; demographics of 27, 39; expectations from 36; historical systems and structures 47; institutions of 8, 41, 135; organizational structure 45–7; post-Great Recession modern era in 21; pre-Great Recession modern era in 21; reasons for avoiding risk in 8–9; *see also* demographic reorientation, in higher education; economic reorientation, in higher education; perception of higher education; technological reorientation, in higher education
high-impact practices 29, 42, 45, 82, 106
high-impact uncertainty 42–3
HIPs *see* high-impact practices
"holding space" 123
Hrabowski, Freeman 142
Huber, Sonya 72
humanities degree, pessimism over practicality of 22
Huston, Therese 5

"ice breaker" activities and exercises 89
imaging of first class 3–4
"immaculate curriculum" 141
implicit biases 39
"imposter syndrome" 5
inclusion 50–1, 61, 83, 87, 118
Indigenous Ecological Knowledge Systems 104
indoor classrooms, learning inside 97–8, 101; productive and efficient 110, 113; risks involved in leaving 112, 141; structure and routine of 107
infantilism 51
informal learning 46, 102
information 23, 25, 49, 103, 115, 121, 138
innovation 27, 29–30, 33, 79, 135, 141–4, 145
innovators 140
inquiry-based learning 86
institutional leaders 135–7, 139; to be still in uncertainty 139–40; focusing on process 139; focus on why 137–8
Integrated Course Design: basic components of 85; framework of 84–6, *85*
integrated learning outcomes 128–9
integrations 88–9, 92–3, 120, 127
integrative learning 89
intellectual uncertainty 62
internet 25
internships 36, 38, 42–6, 43, 46, 69, 82, 86, 89, 91, 98, 102, 129
interviewing 91
investment 8, 20, 21, 89–90, 137

job-shadowing experience 91
Johnson, James 26

Kalikow, Theo 41
knowledge 25, 31, 36, 48, 59, 62, 100–1, 103, 121, 124
Kuh, George 42–3

lakebed sediment study 100
Lang, James 81
leadership 24, 45, 93, 136, 140, 142; armored 71–2; daring 71–2; relational 143–5
leading through uncertainty, principles for 136; analogy of elephant and rider 143–4; be still 138–40; change and enemy of good 140–3; relationships 143–5; start with why 137–8
learning 6; contexts, student response to 49–50; experiences 7, 29, 45, 59, 67, 101–2, 106, 108; management systems 7; risk 7; *see also* out-of-class teaching and learning
"learning artifacts" 121
learning environments 58, 77–8, 80, 89, 122; changing nature of 29–30; resembling world of wicked problems 32–3; risky and safe 50–2; "safetyism" 51
Learning Forum 87–8

152

INDEX

LeBlanc, Paul 24
lecturing 79, 80
Lee, Dorothy 32
Lenox, Michael 33
"less is more," design principle of 110
letter grade system *see* grading
Lewin, Kurt 50
liberal and conservative tendencies, tension between 47
low-stakes practice 91, 119
Lundy, Kasia 135

"Magic Bus Ticketing" 28
massive open online course 22
Mayer, John 143
McDermott, Ray 117
McTighe, Jay 84
meat-packing industry, grade system introduced to 117
mental health crises 31
metacognition 89
millennials 20, 40
modern career development theory 38
Monster Under the Bed (Botkin and Davis) 25
MOOC *see* massive open online course
mountaineering training course 52–3
Mount Holyoke College faculty 117
murder mystery assignment 124, 130
Murphy, Jerome 143
Mushroom at the End of the World, The (Tsing) 27

neighborhood "needing our help," framing 108
New Education, The (Davidson) 116
New Zealand 6, 9, 13–14, 69, 97, 101, 109
noneducative frames 101
"nontraditional students" 26
nontraditional teaching 79
non-White student population, growth of 26–7

off-campus study 6, 12, 14, 69, 101–3, 105, 106, 109–10
"off-syllabus" learning activities 45
one-room schoolhouse 98
online distance learning 18, 24, 101, 133, 135
open-endedness 45
organizational structure, in higher education 45–7
out-of-class teaching and learning 98; activity trap 110; "alternative campus tour" 103;

benefits of 101; challenges associated with 98, 99, 107–8; chemistry 99; communities as classrooms 102–3; faculty encouraging 98–9; framing 108–9; institution-wide approaches to 98; lakebed sediment study 100; "less is more," design principle of 110; pottery analysis 100; public health course 101; reflection of 111–12; Southwest Field Studies 103–7; starting 100; time commitments and structure 101
overframing 108–9
overprotection of students 51

Palmer, Parker 5–6, 66, 143
pedagogical innovation 79
pedagogies 12, 22, 25, 82, 99, 103, 107, 112, 126
"Pedagogies of Place" class 111
peer-to-peer collaboration 43
perception of higher education 5, 11, 20–2, 50, 139; academic disciplines and enrollments 22; changes in 20–1
perfectionism 71, 140
pet therapy 92–3
physical responses to stress 52
place-based learning 23
planned happenstance 38
playground project: completion of 61; fundraising for 60–1; idea pitched by Ritz 57–8; initial skepticism about 59, 60; learning from 61; "problematizing" 59–60; scope and scale of 60; selection of 58–61; students deliberated on 58
"Playlist for Uncertainty" 82; "Common Traps" 92–4; "Designing for Uncertainty" 83–7; "Facilitating for Uncertainty" 87–92
population: growth 26; shifts 26
pottery analysis 100
poverty, as wicked problem 30
practicums 102
pre-orientation backpacking program 16–17
pre-tenure faculty 8, 11
productive emotion 52
productive failure 118–19
productive risk 54, 85, 94, 137
productive risk-taking 135
productive uncertainty 11, 83
professional development opportunity 68–9
project-based learning 12, 79, 82

153

INDEX

racial injustice 18–19, 30, 54
racial justice movement 138
racial reckoning 129, 134, 139
reflection 111–12, 121
Reis, Rick 64
relational leadership 145
relationships 143–5
reopening schools, risks associated with 8
repetition, discipline of 138
reputational ranking scores, refusing to participate in 8
Richmond 61, 69
risk: avoiding 8–9; negative frame of 8; and opportunity, connections between 9–11; perception of 10–11; secondary definition of 9; as weighted term 10
risk-averse organizational culture 8
risk-taking for faculty members 12, 14, 33, 64, 67, 70, 89, 135–6, 140, 142; backwards redesign 84; challenges to dominant paradigms 63; consequences to 67; course redesign 69–70
risky assessment 131; art of failing forward 122–3; authenticity and audience in 126–7; designing for 119–21; integrated learning outcomes 128–9; iteration 121; student choice for 123–5; taking ownership of learning 125–6; *see also* assessment
risky behaviors 8
risky learning 11–13; *see also* risky teaching
risky pass 68–70
risky teaching 49, 72, 107, 109, 118; definition of 11, 14; fundamental part of 5; integrated learning outcomes 128; and learning 11–14, 49–50, 59, 71; relational 129; relevance, challenge, and integration issues in 92–3; time management issues in 93–4; *see also* course design, for uncertainty; course redesign; facilitation of uncertain learning; leading through uncertainty, principles for
Rittell, Horst 30–1
Ritz, Denise 57–8, 60
Robbins, Tony 81
Roth, Michael 50–1

"safe enough" spaces 51–3
safe pedagogical paths: opportunity costs of 68; reasons for selecting 61, 67, 68

"safe space," notion of 50–1
"safetyism" 51
"same ten people" (STPs) 139
scene survey 138–9
self-control 58
self-uncertainty, faculty experiences with 62, 64–7, 73
Selingo, Jeff 141
sense of ownership: in assessment 123, 125–6; collective 87
sense of well-being and college experience, link between 43–4
separation, Albrecht's description of 65
serendipity and career development 38
service learning 12, 43, 82, 85, 92–3, 98, 102, 106
shadow syllabus 72–3
Sinek, Simon 137
skill development 22, 37, 92
"small ball" concept 81
Small Teaching (Lang) 81–2
smart devices and online learning 24
social learning 29
social media 31
Southern New Hampshire University 24
Southwest Field Studies 103–7
Start With Why (Sinek) 137
state funding 21, 118
STEM fields 120
"strange-land experiences" 69
stress, neuroscience of 91
student-centered paradigm 86
student experiences: choice of major and job, link between 37; high-impact practices 42–3; summer internship 36–7; with uncertainty 38–9
student-faculty interaction 42–3
students: adaptations to meet needs of 41; assumptions and expectations about 39; choice 123–7; club leadership 102; debt 20; educational malpractice of blaming 41; and faculty experience, balance between 59; success 41, 117–18, 123, 142; values, ideals, and preferences 40
study abroad 43
study away 86, 102, 106, 110
summative assessment 122–3
supply chain management 36
SWFS *see* Southwest Field Studies

INDEX

tablets and smartphones 24
Taylor, Breanna 18
teacher performance review process 67
teacher-student relationships 45, 50
teaching: assumptions about 4–5; environments, changing nature of 29–30; as performance 6; "teaching as telling" mode 5; traditional 79, 80
teaching methods: educational effectiveness of 80; list of 79
teaching risk: being wrong 6; imposter syndrome 4–5; knowing a lot and getting the content right 6; pedagogical risk 6–7
Teaching What You Don't Know (Therese) 5
Teagle Foundation 69
Teagle project 70
Teagle Teaching Fellow 63
team-based learning 48–9
Team Magic Bus Hult Prize 28–30
technological reorientation, in higher education 22–5; with global pandemic 25; by internet age 24–6; learning platforms 23; online classes 22–3
technology 22–5, 30, 40, 135
technophobia 25
Theirs-Ours-Theirs model 88–9
Thompson, Gordon 4
Thrun, Sebastian 22
Thunberg, Greta 31
time management 93–4
tongue-in-cheek rule 80
traditional classroom assignments 93
traditional teaching 79, 80
training *vs.* education 37
transformative learning 50
treaty workshop 13–14
Tsing, Anna 27
Turning To One Another: Simple Conversations to Restore Hope in the Future (Margaret) 17–18
type 1 uncertainty 38
type 2 uncertainty 38
type 3 uncertainty 38–9

UbD *see* Understanding by Design
UMBC *see* University of Maryland Baltimore County
uncertain learning environments: advantages of 45; course design importance in 83

uncertain teacher 61–4
uncertainties 7–12, 16–17, 19, 29, 31–3, 36–7, 41, 43, 45, 47–9, 51, 53–5, 57, 59–66, 68–74, 75, 78–90, 92–113, 116, 118, 120, 122, 124, 126, 128, 130; categories of 38–9; of Covid-19 global pandemic 9; definition of 9; as desirable condition for career 38; faced by students in college 38; positive and creative qualities of 9–10; small and big 10
uncertainty in learning 11, 32–3, 48, 82, 84, 93; *see also* risky teaching
uncertainty in teaching 7, 61, 64, 81, 90; sensory playground project 58–61; *see also* course design, for uncertainty; course redesign; risky teaching
under-framing 109
Understanding by Design 65, 84
"ungrading" 119
United States: environmental history 114–15, 131; voter participation ranking of 112
"Universities of Nowhere" 103
University of Maryland Baltimore County 142
university organizational structure design challenges 45–7; distribution of classes 46; formal curriculum 46; internships 46; liberal and conservative tendencies, tension between 47; system of record 46–7
unplanned events 38
unproductive stress 52
US Geological Survey "quad" maps 16–17
US News and World Report (*USNWR*) rankings: attempts to challenge power of 8–9; costs of pulling out of 9
Utah, pre-orientation backpacking program in 16–17

volatile, uncertain, complex, and ambiguous situation 134
voter participation ranking of US 112
VUCA scenario *see* volatile, uncertain, complex, and ambiguous situation
vulnerability, in classroom 5
vulnerable teacher 71–73

Warren Wilson College 134
Weaver, Gabriella 126–7
Webber, Melvin 30–1

INDEX

Wheatley, Margaret 17
When Things Fall Apart (Pema) 14
wicked problems 30–2, 147; approach to solve 31; definition of 30; global pandemic 30–1; mental health crises 31; poverty as 30; racial injustice 30
Wiggins, Grant 84

workplace engagement: and college experience, link between 43–4; and well-being 44–5
work-study programs 102
World War II, women and African American students after 41

"Year of the MOOC" 22

Printed in the United States
by Baker & Taylor Publisher Services